Toward Super-Creativity - Improving Creativity in Humans, Machines, and Human - Machine Collaborations

Edited by Sílvio Manuel Brito

Published in London, United Kingdom

IntechOpen

Supporting open minds since 2005

Toward Super-Creativity - Improving Creativity in Humans, Machines, and Human - Machine Collaborations
http://dx.doi.org/10.5772/intechopen.73466
Edited by Sílvio Manuel Brito

Contributors
Teboho Pitso, Wesley Carpenter, Ikenna Emmanuel Onwuegbuna, Luigi Nasta, Luca Pirolo, Margarida Romero, Neta Kela, Itai Kela, Sílvio Manuel Da Rocha Brito

First published in London, United Kingdom, 2020 by IntechOpen
IntechOpen is the global imprint of INTECHOPEN LIMITED, registered in England and Wales, registration number: 11086078, 7th floor, 10 Lower Thames Street, London, EC3R 6AF, United Kingdom
Printed in Croatia

British Library Cataloguing-in-Publication Data
A catalogue record for this book is available from the British Library

Additional hard and PDF copies can be obtained from orders@intechopen.com

Toward Super-Creativity - Improving Creativity in Humans, Machines, and Human - Machine Collaborations
Edited by Sílvio Manuel Brito
p. cm.
Print ISBN 978-1-78985-909-6
Online ISBN 978-1-78985-910-2
eBook (PDF) ISBN 978-1-78985-911-9

For EU product safety concerns:
IN TECH d.o.o., Prolaz Marije Krucifikse Kozulić 3, 51000 Rijeka, Croatia, info@intechopen.com or visit our website at intechopen.com.

Meet the editor

Sílvio Brito holds a degree in Human Resource Management and Work Psychology from ISLA (Higher Institute of Administration and Languages, University of Lisbon), a master's degree in Management (Organizational Behavior) from the Universidade Lusíada, and a PhD in Psychology from the University of Extremadura, Spain. He is a scientific editor for IntechOpen publishing and a member of the Portuguese Society of Psychology and the International Association of Educational Psychology for Children, Youth, Elderly, and Disabled people (INFAD) in Spain. He is also a researcher at the Psyche-EX Research Center of the University of Extremadura. He was a member of the scientific committee of the First International Congress of Entrepreneurs of the University of Salamanca, and is a collaborator for its summer school in the Chair of Entrepreneurs. He was the Vice-President of the Association for Training, Research and Development of Entrepreneurship Behavior in the School of Management at the Polytechnic Institute of Tomar, and was a DoinGlobal collaborator in entrepreneurship. He has been a member of doctoral and master jury commissions in Portugal (IPL, IPS, IPT, ISLA) and abroad (USAL, UNEX), and has supervised various research programs, projects, and internships. He has authored several scientific publications, both national and foreign, in the area of human resources and psychology, namely in the area of entrepreneurship. He is a collaborating member of the journals *Current Psychology* and *Personnel Psychology*. He collaborated in a project to read the scientific blog "Empreender." He was an advisor to the Directorate of the Cooperativa de Ensino Universidade Lusíada, CRL (current Minerva Foundation), Trainer of the CNAF/GUÈRIN Training Center, and Human Resources Technician for the Central Mutual Agricultural Credit Fund.

Contents

Preface XI

Section 1
Creativity in Humans 1

Chapter 1 3
Introductory Chapter: Super Creativity—Mind, Men, and Machine
by Sílvio Manuel da Rocha Brito

Chapter 2 11
The Aha! Moment: The Science Behind Creative Insights
by Wesley Carpenter

Chapter 3 25
Crowdsourcing in the Fashion Industry
by Luigi Nasta and Luca Pirolo

Chapter 4 43
From Individual Creativity to Team-Based Creativity
by Margarida Romero

Section 2
Creativity in Machines 53

Chapter 5 55
Shared Futures: An Exploration of the Collaborative Potential of Intelligent Machines and Human Ingenuity in Cocreating Value
by Teboho Pitso

Section 3
Creativity and Human - Machine Collaborations 79

Chapter 6 81
Diginalysis: The Man-Machine Collaboration in Music Analysis
by Ikenna Emmanuel Onwuegbuna

Chapter 7 89
The Machine-Human Collaboration in Healthcare Innovation
by Neta Kela-Madar and Itai Kela

Preface

Toward Super-Creativity - Improving Creativity in Humans, Machines, and Human–Machine Collaborations is organized into three sections. In the first section, we focus on the creativity of humans and the related cognitive principles and tools that people must have when they make decisions and solve problems. In addition, we tackle how to increase creative mind skills and develop lateral knowledge at work and in society, as well as how to reconcile creativity and individual personality.

In the second section, we focus on the creativity of machines and their ubiquity and influence in different areas. We discuss foundations and theories, the role of machines in human tasks and skills development, and provide insights into artificial intelligence and digital devices and their consequences on human behaviour.

In the third section, we view a practical and theoretical approach to human interaction with machines to create economic, health, social and political benefits, promoting innovation in change and the wellbeing of societies.

Silvio Manuel Brito
Senior Teacher,
Professor of Creativity,
Polytechnic Institute of Tomar,
Tomar, Portugal

Section 1

Creativity in Humans

Chapter 1

Introductory Chapter: Super Creativity—Mind, Men, and Machine

Sílvio Manuel da Rocha Brito

1. Considerations and trends

Creativity is a much-requested attitude nowadays that anything and anyone can pass without it. More than this, it turns in a way of life, fundamentally in investigation tasks, in the business procedures, in the family environment, in the learning processes and health diagnosis, and in all aspects of our daily routines. Thus, to increase this, there is the necessity to conjugate synergies of three elements: the mind, the men, and the machines.

Over the mind, since the concept has undergone several evolutions, its considerations constitute a unique basis for understanding creativity, pointing to emotional orientation and triggering mental activities particularly a threat to the use of common sense. So, creativity appears in a relationship experiences' board [1].

The mind experiences are free and transmit us how versatile the mind is; it considers construction and reconstruction of their presuppositions and the way that generate and self-generate their thoughts in a dual kind of wandering: novelty and utility. So, the creator is the wonder-minded subject [2].

This relationship has been expressed in learning processes, mainly in idea creations, decision-making, problem-solving, lateral thinking, and thought movement [3]. This kind of movement is essentially cultural, an extended process that comports kinetic behavior with mind and culture [4].

But the same relationship represents critical thinking, a form to understand different cultural contexts, an association between thinking measures, like fluency, flexibility, originality, elaboration, and creativity, but only during a performance process [5].

Incidentally, this is confirmed in two experiences where the activity is fundamental to develop a creative mind [6].

This can be enhanced by an unbelieving process, developing creativity in several domains. Between an emotional complex form and a thinking way [7], and by another hand, enhanced by our mind wandering [2] constituting a strong ability to make connections in our whole brain with the purpose of empowering relationships reinforcing the creativity [8].

About a person, we can transform a subject into a creative person, to learn and acquiring personalities such as curiosity, cognition, soft skills, feelings, and motivation; to develop a humanistic vision and to develop personal qualities [9] like research and development [10], working in what he or she views as a challenge and in several domains and activities namely creativity achievements [11].

Furthermore, if we specify abstract concepts, probably we do the lateral thinking [12] in many domains better, and some of them are in verbal expressions [13], innovation tactics [14], environment [15], teamwork [16], leadership expectations [17], and organizational [18] and approach-oriented [19] performances.

If we use the positive mind, we develop creativity, in an equal form, as a man, a person, and a sameness, with positive thinking, and develop and increase creativity by regulating creative emotions [20], but we use also the awe, and by using it, we enhance the creative thinking and control several emotions by positively stimulating the creativity in many perspectives [7]. This will impulse to increase one of the most important personality factors to be creative, present in most studies in this area [21].

But the creativity as a human, personal, and intimate human attitude depends essentially on the will. New theories approach this reality, and one of them is a "triangular theory," where creative subjects challenge other common people's beliefs and share an unconscious and conscious reality vision and, in face of this, there originates different combinations of challenge types, creativity materialized examples [22].

According to all this, any human is a creative person [23].

About a machine, with the fast technological development in a brief future, we suppose, there will be difficulty in dating a man from a machine and vice versa. Thus, artificial intelligence is the mainly example in moral decisions, which helps us in making ethical decisions about our expectations; for example, being a part of a platform that helps us to make decisions on the use of autonomous vehicles [24] and health preservation where certain human body organs are changed by bionic devices [25] such as legs, tissues, bones, exoskeletons, and much more.

So, this symbiosis [26] is intense and very creative in such a way that, increases the development of human performance at work, as well as occupational health and individual behavior in general, and artificial intelligence is living in ourselves either [27]. In many aspects, especially in a culture, that we can say that we are living an authentic cyberculture paradigm [28]. As mankind progresses with the machine, it also progresses in the new competencies' acquisition, the ignition competence being the creativity attitude [29].

Therefore, the psychological concept of creativity is daily changing, since it is a non-rational and inflexible concept, on the contrary, it rests in intervisibility and in a world where the intellectual heritage belongs to machines; the last word in creative actions belongs to humans [30].

The definition of creative activity is *any kind of creativity that creates something new, be it anything from the outside world, a product of the creative activity, or an organization of thought or feeling that acts and is present in man himself* [31].

Creativity activity is not the same as "creative thinking"; it means interaction between a sociocultural context and the mind of people. It is a systemic phenomenon, more than individual [32]; this is seen as the production of anything new that has a significant impact on a given field and is widely recognized and valued through the demonstration of its social usefulness. In the lower case or in superior case [33], the social significance of the materialized idea depends on what people can do with it.

So, creativity is a systemic process that arises from the relationship between different kinds of actions (individual, field, and domain) that are in different contexts (personal background, society and culture, economy, and globalization) that affect them, as shown in **Figure 1** [34].

According to **Figure 1**, from the "individual" point of view, it is necessary to analyze the cultural and social contexts in which this individual operates. The interaction between the individual domains favours the communication transmission, and the interaction between the individual field stimulates the result occurrence with the original potential, producing and stimulating novelty, where the interaction between "field" and "domain" selects novelty by judgment and selection of creative results.

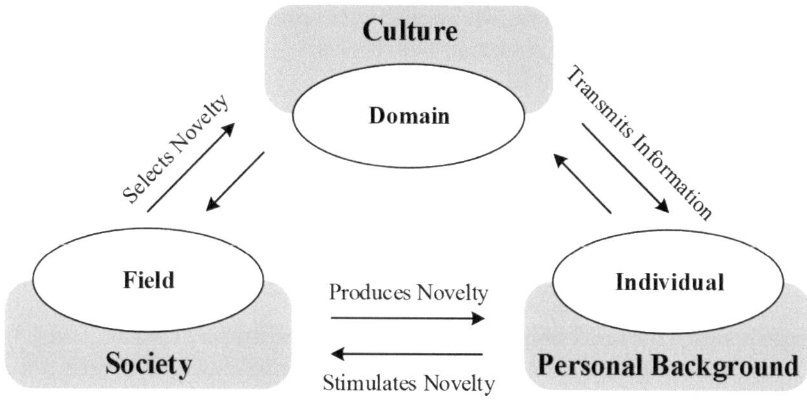

Figure 1.
Creativity Systemic Process. Source: Adapted from Csikszentmihalyi [34].

This triangulation of perspectives and interpretations reflects the senses of what can search to be faced as "new" trough a confrontation os questions and answers between creativity researchers and participants [35] where the active mind is always present.

Some models mean the presence of the man and the machine, where the computational reports contribute to human insights and establish the relationship with the human neural system to quantify the creativity quality levels and the divergence or convergence of creative thinking, giving an integrative perspective of creativity and contribute for developing the creative cognition [36].

All this have the aim to empower creativity in the work conditions on high-tech environments and the collaborator's health, through the optimization of work dimensions as work atmosphere, vertical collaboration, autonomy and freedom, respect, alignment, and lateral collaboration, so creativity emerges from a good climate, management, and knowledge strategy [37].

2. Challenges and proposals

Following these purposes, this single book reveals itself in an interesting vision in how the relational trilogy between humanity, its knowledge, and the use of the machine responds to the challenges placed before it, with respect to the own fears and preoccupations, to the human nature and to its social purpose, as well as to the synergy strategic management between man and machine, and to the results' unpredictable impact.

Like the trilogy mind, men, and machine, this book proposes three moments: the first moment deals with the creativity in humans that suggest what they can do and what they do by doing this. The second moment deals with the creativity in the machines, that is to say, the way in which they propose to the man to develop their capacities. The third moment deals with the collaboration between man and machine interaction.

Therefore, we begin with a spectacular article from Prof. Wesley Carpenter that talks about the power of a special cognitive moment, which conducts a cognitive mutation that will result in creativity, especially on problem-solving and critical solutions. Next, we have an article no less interesting, by Dr Luigi Nasta and Dr Luca Pirolo, who moves us to the fashion world, in a curious form of innovation to increase and improve the commercial relationship form, between fashion companies and customers, in a crowdsourcing operation.

Through the second moment, Dr. Teboho Pitso presents us a wonderful study about the influence of intelligent machines' capacities versus the human's cognition and the use of both in creating value.

The last moment is marked by a special and critical work by Dr. Ikkena Onwuegbuna on the machine incidence in musical creation, and how it can be productive if it interacts with the subject with regard to a process of analysis.

Finally, we finish with a wonderful proposal by Dr. Niki Lambaropoulos, who brings us an innovative project—an adaptive virtual reality brain-computer interfaces, which is very useful for the search of new solutions and for learning new tasks.

In conclusion, this book helps us to understand the union of the real with the virtual, through the connecting link that leads to change and evolve: creativity at its best! Surely, it will be a friend, really good, to have in the pocket or on the head table, which opens the vision for a new time, a new place, and a new world scenario!

Author details

Sílvio Manuel da Rocha Brito[1,2,3]

1 Polytechnic Institute of Tomar, Portugal

2 Entrepreneurship Promotion and Development Association (EPDA), Spain

3 Psique-Ex, Extremadura University, Spain

*Address all correspondence to: silvio.brito@ipt.pt

References

[1] Spearman C. Creative Mind. The Journal of Nervous and Mental Disease. December 1931;**74**(6):783

[2] Fox KC, Beaty RE. Mind-wandering as creative thinking: Neural, psychological, and theoretical considerations. Current Opinion in Behavioral Sciences. 2019;**27**:123-130. DOI: 10.1016/j.cobeha.2018.10.009

[3] Molaei S, Fini S, Rahmani MN. The role of creative minds (creativity) in the process of academic achievement. Iranian Journal of Positive Psychology. 2018;**4**(1):27-31. ISSN: 2423-6985

[4] Glăveanu VP. The cultural basis of the creative process: A dual-movement framework. The Creative Process, Palgrave Studies in Creativity and Culture. 2018;**4**:297-316. DOI: 10.1057/978-1-137-50563-7_12

[5] Wechsler SM, Saiz C, Rivas SF, Vendramini CMM, Almeida LS, Mundim MC, et al. Creative and critical thinking: Independent or overlapping components? Thinking Skills and Creativity. 2018;**27**:114-122. DOI: 10.1016/j.tsc.2017.12.003

[6] Main KJ, Aghakhani H, Labroo AA, Greidanus NS. Change it up: Inactivity and repetitive activity reduce creative thinking. The Journal of Creative Behavior. 2018;**0**(0):1-12. DOI: 10.1002/jocb.373

[7] Chirico A, Glaveanu VP, Cipresso P, Riva G, Gaggioli A. Awe enhances creative thinking: An experimental study. Creativity Research Journal. 2018;**30**(2):123-131. DOI: 10.1080/10400419.2018.1446491

[8] Beaty RE, Kenett YN, Christensen AP, Rosenberg MD, Benedek M, Chen Q, et al. Robust prediction of individual creative ability from brain functional connectivity. Proceedings of the National Academy of Sciences. 2019;**115**(5):1087-1092. DOI: 10.1073/pnas.1713532115

[9] Richards R. Everyday creativity and the healthy mind. In: Creative Person, Palgrave Studies in Creativity and Culture. 2018. pp. 135-152. DOI: 10.1057/978-1-137-55766-7_9

[10] Hazak A, Ruubel R, Virkebau M. When would creative R&D employees like to work? International Journal of Organizational Analysis. 2019. DOI: 10.1108/ijoa-04-2018-1409. Downloaded by 81.22.47.68 At 21:12 13 January 2019 (PT)

[11] Diedrich J, Jauk E, Silvia PJ, Gredlein JM, Neubauer AC, Benedek M. Assessment of real-life creativity: The Inventory of Creative Activities and Achievements (ICAA). Psychology of Aesthetics, Creativity, and the Arts. 2018;**12**(3):304-316

[12] Ezzat H, Agogué M, Le Masson P, Weil B, Cassotti M. Specificity and abstraction of examples: Opposite effects on fixation for creative ideation. The Journal of Creative Behavior. 2018;**0**(0):1-8. DOI: 10.1002/jocb.349

[13] Piirto J. The creative process in writers. The Creative Process, Palgrave Studies in Creativity and Culture. 2018;**6**:89-121. DOI: 10.1057/978-1-137-50563-7_4

[14] Nilsson ÅW, Jahnke M. Tactics for norm-creative innovation. She Ji: The Journal of Design, Economics, and Innovation. 2018;**4**(4):375-391. DOI: 10.1016/j.sheji.2018.11.002

[15] Richards R. Everyday creativity and the healthy mind. Palgrave Studies in Creativity and Culture. 2018;**7**:153-170. DOI: 10.1057/978-1-137-55766-7_10

[16] Fong PSW, Men C, Luo J, Jia R. Knowledge hiding and team

creativity: The contingent role of task interdependence. Management Decision. 2018;**56**(2):329-343. DOI: 10.1108/md-11-2016-0778

[17] Adil MS, Hamid KBA. The relationships between leader creativity expectations, intrinsic motivation, and creative performance. SEISENSE Journal of Management. 2019;**2**(2):58-68. DOI: 10.33215/sjom.v2i2.123

[18] Kaufman JC. Uniquely creative: Developing a new outline for positive outcomes. Creativity. Theories - Research - Applications. 2019;**5**(2):188-196. DOI: 10.1515/ctra-2018-0018

[19] Li H, Li F, Chen T. Do performance approach-oriented individuals generate creative ideas? The roles of outcome instrumentality and task persistence. Journal of Applied Social Psychology. 2018;**48**(3):117-127. DOI: 10.1111/jasp.12495

[20] Chiu F-C, Hsu C-C, Lin Y-N, Liu C-H, Chen H-C, Lin C-H. Effects of creative thinking and its personality determinants on negative emotion regulation. Psychological Reports: 003329411877597. 2018;**0**(0):1-28. DOI: 10.1177/0033294118775973

[21] Unsworth K. Creativity in the context of multiple goals. In: Martin L, Wilson N, editors. The Palgrave Handbook of Creativity at Work. 2018. pp. 23-41. DOI: 10.1007/978-3-319-77350-6_2

[22] Sternberg RJ. A triangular theory of creativity. Psychology of Aesthetics, Creativity, and the Arts. 2018;**12**(1):50-67. DOI: 10.1037/aca0000095

[23] Kronfeldner M. Explaining creativity. In: Gaut B, Kieran M, editors. Routledge Handbook on Creativity and Philosophy. New York: Routledge. pp. 213-229

[24] Awad E, Dsouza S, Kim R, Schulz J, Henrich J, Shariff A, et al. The moral machine experiment. Nature. 2018;**563**:59-64. DOI: 10.1038/s41586-018-0637-6

[25] Pagaduan JV, Bhatta A, Romer LH, Gracias DH. 3D hybrid small scale devices. Small. 2018;**14**(27):1702497. DOI: 10.1002/smll.201702497

[26] Mourad S, Tewfik A. Machine assisted human decision making. In: 2018 IEEE International Conference on Acoustics, Speech and Signal Processing (ICASSP); 2018. DOI: 10.1109/icassp.2018.8462087

[27] Nagao K. Symbiosis between humans and artificial intelligence. In: Artificial Intelligence Accelerates Human Learning. Springer; 2019. pp. 135-151. DOI: 10.1007/978-981-13-6175-3_6

[28] Pereira LM. Cyberculture, symbiosis, and syncretism. AI & SOCIETY. 2018;**33**(3):447-452. DOI: 10.1007/s00146-017-0715-6

[29] Leigh S, Agrawal H, Maes P. Robotic symbionts: Interweaving human and machine actions. IEEE Pervasive Computing. 2018;**17**(2):34-43. DOI: 10.1109/mprv.2018.022511241

[30] Richards R. Everyday Creativity and the Healthy Mind: Dynamic New Paths for Self and Society. Oakland: Palgrave/McMillan. 2018. pp. 1-377. DOI: 10.1057/978-1-137-55766-7

[31] Lindqvist G. Vygotsky's theory of creativity. Creativity Research Journal. 2003;**15**(2-3):245-251. DOI: 10.1080/10400419.2003.9651416

[32] Janesick VJ. Intuition and creativity: A pas de deux for qualitative researchers. Qualitative Inquiry. 2001;**7**(5):531-540. DOI: 10.1177/107780040100700501

[33] Boden M. The Creative Mind. 2nd ed. London: Routledge. 2002. 344p. ISBN: 0-203-34008-6

[34] Csikszentmihalyi M. Stalking a new world order. New Literary History. 2004;**35**(2):339-348. DOI: 10.1353/nlh.2004.0029. Project MUSE

[35] Lebuda I, Glăveanu VP. Researching the social in creativity, past, present and future: An introduction to the palgrave handbook of social creativity research. In: The Palgrave Handbook of Social Creativity Research. 2018. pp. 1-9. DOI: 10.1007/978-3-319-95498-1_1

[36] Mekern V, Hommel B, Sjoerds Z. Computational models of creativity: A review of single-process and multi-process recent approaches to demystifying creative cognition. Current Opinion in Behavioral Sciences. 2019;**27**:47-54. DOI: 10.1016/j.cobeha.2018.09.008

[37] Lapierre J, Giroux V-P. Creativity and work environment in a high-tech context. Creativity and Innovation Management. 2003;**12**(1):11-23. DOI: 10.1111/1467-8691.00263

Chapter 2

The Aha! Moment: The Science Behind Creative Insights

Wesley Carpenter

Abstract

Insight, often referred to as an "aha moment," has been defined as a sudden, conscious change in a person's representation of a stimulus, situation, event, or problem. Recent advances in neuroimaging technology and neurophysiological techniques have allowed researchers an opportunity to hone in on the neural circuitry that governs insight, a phenomenon that has been theorized about by cognitive psychologists for over a century. Studies show that insight is not a sudden flash that comes from nowhere, but in fact is the result of the unconscious mind piecing together loosely connected bits of information stemming from prior knowledge and experiences and forming novel associations among them. This conceptualization of insight naturally gives rise to comparisons between insight and creativity. Creativity, however, involves many cognitive processes, occurring in many regions of the brain and thus cannot be laterally localized as insight can. Thus, creativity is not considered synonymous with insight; however, insight can certainly result in creative solutions during creative problem solving.

Keywords: insight, Aha! moment, eureka, creativity, analytical problem solving, creative problem solving, functional fixedness

1. Introduction

Undoubtedly, we have all had them, that moment of extraordinary clarity in which the solution to a difficult problem suddenly seems to just "pop in there." Or perhaps it is a punchline to a joke that you all of a sudden get, or the perfect metaphor that suddenly comes into awareness. Where do these whiffs of inspiration come from? Do they just magically pop in there, as if given to us by some muse? Or is there perhaps a more scientific explanation? Insight, or an "Aha!" moment as it is commonly referred to, is not mysterious at all. In fact, recent advances in neuroimaging technology have made it seem less mysterious than ever. Insight has been defined as any sudden comprehension, realization, or problem solution that involves a reorganization of the elements of a person's mental representation of a stimulus, situation, or event to yield a nonobvious or nondominant interpretation. Insights may appear suddenly, but are preceded by incremental unconscious processing. Research by cognitive psychologists and cognitive neuroscientists has shown that moments of insight are merely the result of the brain making connections between weakly and strongly activated bits of information, and then bringing them to consciousness.

2. Insight versus analytical problem-solving

Some of the earliest research on insight sought to conclude whether there really was a difference between solving a problem via insight versus solving a problem via a heuristic driven type of problem solving methodology. Firstly, there are definitional differences between the two. Insight, commonly referred to as an "aha moment," has been defined as a sudden, conscious change in a person's representation of a stimulus, situation, event, or problem [1]. It should be noted that insights, while they do suddenly merge into one's stream of consciousness, are proceeded by unconscious processing to arrive at the insight. This is in contrast to analytical problem solving which involves the use of a systematic process or simply logical reasoning to arrive at a solution to a problem. It is deliberate and conscious, and often involves the use of some type of strategy which allow the individual to progress incrementally toward a solution. Because this type of methodology involves storing and manipulating information in the prefrontal cortex utilizing the individuals working memory capacity, individuals can typically fully explain the steps taken to arrive at the solution [2], whereas with insight, individuals cannot readily reconstruct the procedure followed to reach the solution. Albert Einstein summarized the unconscious nature of insight when he said, "At times I feel certain I am right while not knowing the reason" [3].

Differences between the two problem solving methods vary beyond differences in definition and accuracy of solutions, neuroimaging studies suggest that patterns of brain activity during and prior to solving by insight versus analysis are fundamentally different as well [4–6]. This suggests different cognitive strategies are being employed depending upon whether the solution arrives via insight or analytical means. Studies have shown that the brain actually predicts in advance whether the problem will be solved analytically or by insight [6, 7]. For example, Salvi et al. [8] showed that people blink and move their eyes differently prior to solving by insight versus solving analytically.

Other findings using the compound remote associates (CRA) test have provided additional support for the notion that insight processing is qualitatively different from analysis type problem solving. Compound remote associate problems are similar to items on the remote associates test developed by Mednick in 1962. Subjects must produce a solution word (e.g., sweet) that can form compounds with each of three problem words (e.g., tooth, potato, and heart). This type of test, while not considered a classic insight test, often give rise to Aha! moments. They are frequently used when studying creativity, problem solving, and insight.

Bowden and Jung-Beeman [9] presented compound remote associates test problems to participants followed by a single word that they were instructed to verbalize as quickly as possible. This known as cognitive priming. For unsolved problems, following verbalization participants indicated whether the word was the solution to the problem they had just been given. If it was, subjects had to indicate whether this realization had come to them suddenly, which would indicate insight, or incrementally, which would indicate an analytical solution strategy was employed.

Another type of cognitive priming was used to induce abstract thinking in subjects as opposed to concrete thinking by asking subjects to thinking about distant ideas (past or future), remote locations or other's perspectives versus asking subjects to think about ideas related to the here and now. According to construal level theory, increasing the psychological distance, that is, thinking about things that are increasingly far away in space or time or about people that are different from oneself tends to engage abstract thinking [10], which in turn is hypothesized to produce more creative and insightful ideas. Subjects who were primed to think in the abstract by considering ideas at far psychological distances performed better on insight related tasks whereas those primed to think concretely by considering ideas at short psychological distances did considerably better on problems requiring analysis [11].

2.1 Differences in cognitive strategies

A study by Salvi et al. [8] suggest additional evidence that there are differences between insight and analysis problem solving wherein it was revealed that solutions provided by insight were correct more often that solutions garnered by analysis. A possible explanation of this is that insights are typically all or nothing, i.e., there is no intermediate opportunity to alter one's information or solution strategy, ideas, thought processes, etc., when there is a looming deadline whereas analytical problem solving, due to its conscious nature, allows for individuals to make errors of commission, becoming fixated on irrelevant information (i.e., functional fixedness), etc., as a looming deadline approaches [7].

A pattern of errors made by subjects using either of the two methods suggests differences in cognitive strategies for problem solving via insight and analysis. They found that participants who solve predominantly by insight tend to make errors of omission (i.e., time outs) rather than errors of commission, whereas participants who tend to solve analytically make errors of commission rather than errors of omission (i.e., incorrect responses).

3. The neuroscience of insight

Recent technological advances have allowed neuroscientists to begin getting closer to understanding the complex neural underpinnings of the Aha! moment, i.e., insight. Neuroimaging studies on the insight phenomenon typically involve the use of either electroencephalography (EEG) or functional magnetic resonance imaging (fMRI), or commonly a combination of both to investigate the temporal dynamics and neural correlates of insight. Electroencephalography affords the researcher high temporal resolution which provides highly precise time measurements which are necessary to capture the rapidly changing electrical activity in the brain when subjected to stimulation. A disadvantage of EEG, however, is poor spatial resolution. Thus, functional magnetic resonance imaging is commonly used to provide high spatial resolution for precise localization of brain activity. Together these techniques are able to isolate the neural correlates of insight in both space and time.

As discussed above, the development of short compound remote associates problems readily solvable by insight by Bowden and Jung-Beeman has proved useful in neuroscientific studies as well. Early studies of insight typically posed a small number of complex problems to participants. Most participants take many minutes to solve such problems, when they are able to solve them at all. However, neuroimaging and electrophysiological methods require many trials to accurately record brain activity. Compound remote associates problems are well suited to neuroimaging and electrophysiological studies.

These types of problems afford the researcher two primary advantages. First, they can be solved via insight or through analysis. Furthermore, each problem presented, whether solved with insight or analysis, does not differ in complexity or solving duration [2, 12]. Essentially, this test controls for all confounding variables for the actual cognitive strategy used, therefore whether insight or analysis was used can be more easily identified without error. Secondly, a response utilizing either method can be given relatively quickly, thereby allowing a large number of trials per condition in a short time period [7].

As described above, each compound-remote-associates problem consists of three words (e.g., potato, tooth, heart). Participants are instructed to think of a single word that can form a compound or familiar two-word phrase with each of the three problem words (e.g., sweet can join with potato, tooth, and heart to form sweet potato, sweet tooth, and sweetheart). The instant subjects think of the word that can combine with all three, they press a button as quickly as possible. Subjects are instructed to not take any time to analyze the solution, simply press the button as soon as they become aware of the solution. They are then prompted to verbalize the solution and then to press a button to indicate whether that solution had popped into awareness suddenly (insight) or whether the solution had resulted from a more methodical hypothesis-testing approach.

When participants indicated that the solution had popped into awareness suddenly, thus indicating insight, the EEG showed a burst of high-frequency gamma waves over the right temporal lobe (just above the right ear in the right hemisphere) as shown in **Figure 1**, and the fMRI showed a corresponding change in blood flow in the medial aspect of the right anterior superior temporal gyrus (aSTG) [4]. No gamma wave activity was reported in the left hemisphere. This activity in the right hemisphere (RH) is interpreted as the sudden availability of the solution coming into consciousness, i.e., the Aha! moment.

The spatial and temporal correspondence of the EEG and fMRI signals suggests they were triggered by the same underlying neural event [13]. Activity was also reported in the bilateral hippocampus, para-hippocampal gyri and anterior and posterior cingulate cortex, but further studies suggest activity in these areas were relatively weak compared to the strong signals produced in the right anterior superior temporal gyrus. Moreover, the signal produced in the right temporal region of the brain occurred nearly the same time as when subjects realized the solution to each of the problems; the same region that is implicated in other tasks requiring semantic integration [14]. Furthermore, high frequency gamma-wave signals have been proposed to be a mechanism for assimilating and ultimately making connections among information as it emerges into consciousness [15].

Figure 2 highlights differences in EEG power just before, during and after the solution to the problem was given by the individual. The figure clearly shows

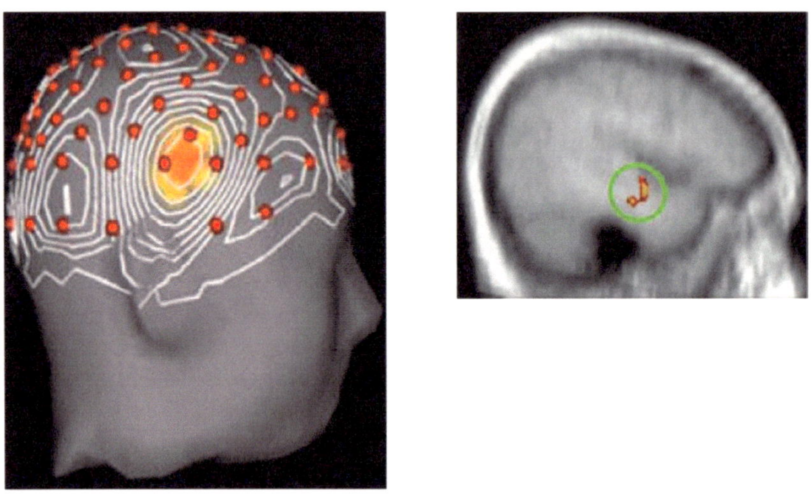

Figure 1.
The image on the left shows a topographic distribution of gamma-band activity during the insight solutions and the image on the right shows area of activation corresponding to insight effect during functional magnetic resonance imaging (fMRI). Adapted from Kounios and Beeman [13].

a distinct difference in EEG power when the participant reported a solution via insight whereas virtually no change in EEG power when a solution was arrived at via an analysis type of problem solving method. Thus, clear differences in neural activity just before a solution comes to consciousness validates distinct differences between solution by insight and solution by analysis. It should be noted that one of the advantages of problem solving via insight is that sometimes it brings nonobvious solutions to problems to conscious awareness. The anterior cingulate cortex (ACC) is thought to prepare the brain for the integration of weakly activated ideas and solutions [5]. When a problem is presented, one's attention is typically dominated by obvious solutions to a given problem, however, if there exists inconsistent or competing information, the ACC is can become activated, and thus allow more distant, weakly activated ideas to come to consciousness.

In addition to the increase in gamma wave activity, **Figure 3** shows a sudden increase in power in the alpha-band frequency occurred about 1.5 s before insight solutions, suggesting a decrease in neural activity within the right visual cortex. These effects are not attributable to emotional responses, because the neural activity preceded the solutions. Alpha waves reflect cortical deactivation or inhibition of certain brain areas [5], thus the increase in alpha waves just before solution is analogous to looking away, closing one's eyes, or looking up at the ceiling, all of

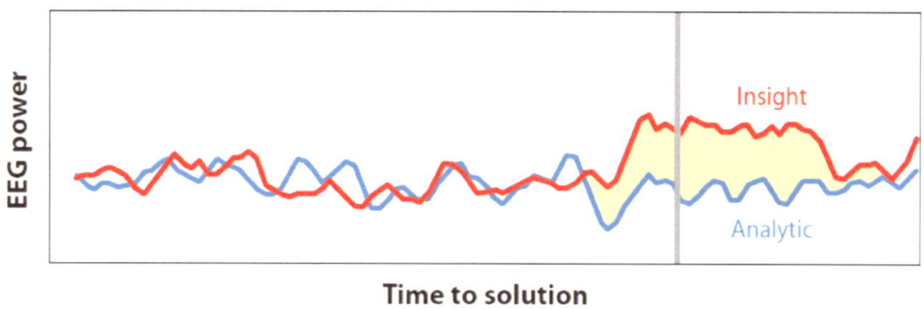

Figure 2.
Time course of insight- and analysis-related gamma-band EEG power. Adapted from Kounios and Beeman [38].

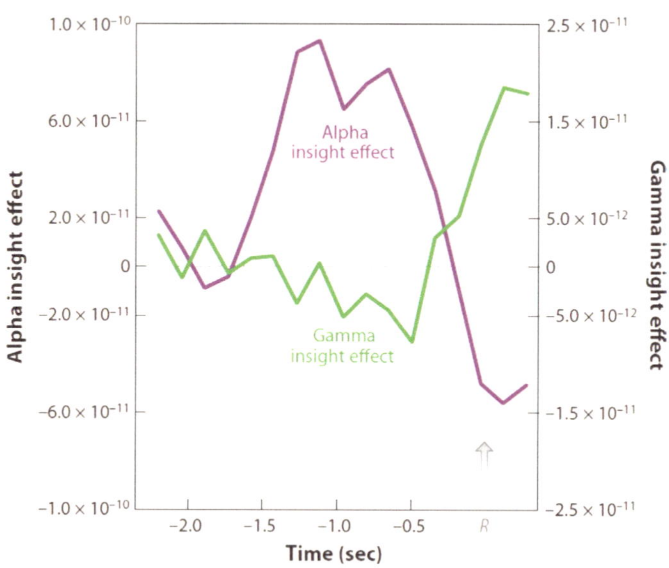

Figure 3.
Graph showing large increase of power in the alpha-band frequency just prior to increase in gamma band activity, known as the alpha insight effect. Adapted from Kounios and Beeman [38].

which are common tactics employed by individuals to minimize visual distractions when solving problems. The burst of alpha waves and then gamma waves suggest before insight solutions suggest the brain is changing the focus of its efforts to limit visual distractions thereby facilitating the integration of remote semantic elements and allowing a pathway for it to emerge into conscious awareness. This is in contrast to solutions produced via analysis which shows increased neural activity (i.e., decreased alpha-band activity) in the visual cortex. A decrease in alpha waves indicates a response to demands on one's attention, thus the decrease in alpha waves suggests subjects were focusing on the external environment while solving problems rather than making attempts to minimize distractions.

The primary take-away appears to be that a subject's neural activity during resting state, i.e., task-free state, prior to each compound remote associates problem suggest that distinct patterns of neural activity precede problems that people eventually solve by insight versus those solved by analysis. These changes in the brains resting state prior to solving insight problems suggest it is possible to predict a priori whether a subject is likely to use insight to solve a problem rather than analysis.

4. The psychology of insight

The neuroscientific view of insight allows to understand the neurological processes that underpin the moment of insight, but what exactly is insight from a cognitive psychology point of view? Indeed, Aha! moments are one of the most intriguing and unexplained processes of the human mind [16]. From a cognitive psychology perspective, attempting to place the insight phenomena into a proper theoretical framework to provide scientifically valid explanations of why the insight phenomena occurs has been difficult.

Famous American psychologist William James [17] put forth the first psychological theory of insight known as the associationist theory of insight which proposed that new ideas are combinations of existing ideas, that sudden insights are merely the result of having a lot of information in being able to make connections between fax. These connections are made during a suitable incubation period, an unguided, unconscious process whereby individuals simply take time off from the problem. A competing view of insight was put forth by the German Gestaltist Karl Duncker who was attempting to explain the psychology of insight and thus put forth proper definition of insight [18]. The Gestalt view of insight described it as "a process based on reconstructing the core of a problem, rethinking its basic assumptions and originating a new and creative solution, a process usually occurring in an unexpected and unpredictable manner" [19, 20].

The Gestalt view of insight differed in that they believed insight problems are solved suddenly and therefore no chain of connections could explain the discovery. This view suggests that insights occur while performing an analysis of the problem in which you are drawn to a potential solution, but then realize it cannot work. This is referred to as an impasse in which your mind becomes fixated on a particular solution and you therefore become incapable of exploring the problem from other angles. The solution arrives not by making incremental associations but by overcoming the fixation thus allowing a restructuring of a problem that allows you to eventually arrive at a solution. Restructuring is conceptualizing the problem differently, essentially seeing the problem in a whole new way, hence the solution is sudden and surprising. Individuals are not consciously aware of how they overcame the problem.

Other theories have been proposed to provide theoretical framework to explain insight. For example, The Progress Monitoring Theory by MacGregor et al. [21], is based on the hill-climbing idea that problem solving proceeds with the problem solver seeking to minimize the gap between the current state of the problem and the goal state. Individuals begin attempting to solve a problem by putting forth what they believe is an informed solution, which is then subsequently altered by making incremental improvements to the solution thereby getting closer and closer to the correct solution. When such incremental improvements do not result in the correct solution, the individual reaches an impasse, often likely due to the individual becoming fixated on an incorrect strategy or incomplete information. Now the individual must search for a new approach to solve the problem. This theory implies that individuals constantly monitor their own progress in order to promptly switch to a different problem-solving strategy in case the current one is not successful. This theory suggests that the Aha! moment may be achieved with an incremental approach, with constant monitoring of one's own cognitive processes as a pivotal feature, making the Aha! moment more like a conscious epiphenomenon of a general problem-solving process rather than a burst of uncommon cognitive processes [22, 23].

In contrast to the Progress Monitoring Theory, Knoblich and colleagues introduced the Representational Change Theory [24] which offered an alternative explanation of how an impasse is overcome, that is, through a reorganization of a problem's representation. Representation can be thought of as the distribution of activation across pieces of knowledge in memory [25]. This theory suggests that the problem is first represented using information or knowledge that is not relevant for the solution, hence an impasse is reached. Once this impasse is reached, the representation is altered such that relevant information becomes active and a viable solution merges into consciousness. Knoblich et al. [24, 26] suggest that the main issue of problem-solving is an individual's tendency to set unnecessary constraints through a very restricted representation of the problem, which is a function of limited, incomplete or ambiguous prior knowledge. Once the impasse is reached, by relaxing the unnecessary constraints that have been placed on the problem by deactivating the recalled knowledge linked to the problem or decomposing elements of the task by dividing it into perceptual chunks, a new representation of the problem can be reached [23, 25].

Progress Monitoring Theory and Representational Change Theory differs primarily in how one deals with an eventual impasse that impedes a solution. Bowden and Beeman have proposed another theoretical framework to explain insight by attempting to link a cognitive psychological model to actual neurological processes within particular regions of the brain. The theory proposes that insights occur when the initial representation of the problem initiates a strong semantic activation of information that allows for the generation of obvious solutions to a problem and a weak (unconscious) semantic activation of remote, alternative information important for the generation of non-obvious solutions to a problem. The weak semantic activation which is responsible for allowing remote associations to be made is thought to be produced in the right hemisphere whereas the strong semantic activation is thought to be produced in the left hemisphere [22]. Initially, solvers may be unable to take advantage of weak solution activation because it is weak, and therefore might be blocked by stronger, more focused, but misdirected semantic activations [22]. A new restructured representation of the problem emerges when integration of weakly activated information and subsequent associations made therein are reinforced, strengthened, and ultimately emerge into consciousness.

It is important to recognize that both hemispheres of the brain involve complimentary processes that work synergistically to produce a solution. Information is shared between the two hemispheres, it is the presence of this laterality that allows the solution to merge into consciousness. However, it is thought that the right hemisphere s predominantly responsible for the generation of non-obvious solutions to a given problem, i.e., creative problem solving. Psychological studies of insight suggest that the good gestalt theory is largely false. The consensus among scholars is that insight is primarily a function of previous experience and acquired knowledge [27]. Rather than a sudden restructuring, the mind seems to gradually get closer to the correct solution. And that's pretty consistent with the association theory and the Bowden and Beeman theory that creativity occurs when existing ideas combine together. The existing ideas on the new metal structure our new, they're familiar ideas and Conventions that are already in the domain and then have been internalized by the creator.

5. The relationship between insight and creativity

One of the most enduring theories of creativity is the Wallas [28] model of creativity. It begins with a preparation stage where the individual properly identifies and defines the problem, and then proceeds to gather information necessary to solve the problem. Next comes incubation which involves taking some time away from a problem to allow the unconscious mind to process the information to produce a solution. This is the state where information is assimilated, and remote associations are thought to be formed [29].

The third stage in the Wallas model is illumination, or more commonly referred to as insight because it results in the familiar Aha! experience. During this stage, a solution suddenly emerges into consciousness, light a lightbulb being turned on. This sudden illumination is still controversial however. Weisberg [30] wrote, "there seems very little reason to believe that solutions to novel problems come about in leaps of insight. At every step of the way, the process involves small movements away from what is known" (p. 50). Perhaps we only perceive it as sudden because the processing that led up to the insight is below conscious awareness [31]. Prominent creativity researcher Sawyer [27] suggests insights only seem sudden because we didn't notice the many incremental steps, or mini-insights, that immediately preceded it. He suggests rather than the familiar light bulb turning on metaphor, perhaps the tip of an iceberg or final brick in the wall is more appropriate.

The final stage was verification. At that point, the individual tests the idea or applies the solution. Although the four stages of the creative process included in the Wallas model are generally accepted to be accurate, it is generally accepted that the creative process is much more recursive than the linear Wallas model is depicted as being. It is worth noting that while other models have dissected the four stages of the Wallas model into further stages, the fundamental four of the Wallas model still remain.

With respect to the second stage of the Wallas stage model of creativity, namely incubation, one of the oldest observations in the psychology of creativity is that a creative idea is often preceded by a period of unconscious incubation [17, 32]. There is much research studying the incubation effect and its relationship with creative insight [16, 33–35]. It is generally agreed upon that there exists an incubation effect, although the exact nature of the associated unconscious processes remains uncertain. Hypotheses include mental relaxation, selective forgetting, random subconscious recombination, and spreading activation.

The relationship between insight and creativity is still a controversial one. Whether insight is a component of creativity (or a component of the creative process), simply a form of problem solving that may or may not produce a creative solution to a given problem [36], or something else entirely is as yet unanswered. Experimental and theoretical work support conflicting views regarding this question [37]. Sternberg and Davidson [16] conceptualized creativity as the ability to change existing thinking patterns, producing something that is useful, novel and generative. One cannot help but notice similarities between this conception of creativity and the generally accepted definition of insight, namely "a reorganization of the elements of a person's mental representation of a stimulus, situation or event to yield a nonobvious or nondominant interpretation" [38]. Thus, it is likely that both conceptions are correct. We know from experience that insight is not always involved in creative problem solving and therefore must not be a necessary component of it. Creative solutions can also arise through a conscious, deliberate analysis of the problem [39].

Creativity and insight have similar neurological correlates as well. Deliberate creativity that results from analysis is primarily controlled by the prefrontal cortex. However, creativity that comes as a sudden flash of insight involves three brain regions, namely the temporal, occipital, and parietal (TOP). Moreover, a prominent view of creativity is that it is based on the processing of remote or loose connections between ideas [40]. Research suggests the brain's right hemisphere is primarily responsible for the processing of remote associations and the brains left hemisphere is responsible for the processing of close or obvious associations [4]. Research suggests it is this rightward asymmetry that allows for weak activation of a broad semantic field, thus allowing for nondominant, remote associations between disparate ideas to take place. Hence the Bowden and Beeman theory seems to provide a neurological basis for Mednick's theory of creativity.

6. Conclusion

Insight is any sudden comprehension, realization, or problem solution that involves a reorganization of the elements of a person's mental representation of a stimulus, situation, or event to yield a nonobvious or nondominant interpretation. Insight is sudden, but it is preceded by incremental unconscious processing, sometimes referred to as mini-insights [27]. This unconscious processing appears to involve the integration of information contained within a weakly activated broad semantic field thus allowing remote associations of knowledge to stream into consciousness culminating in what we often refer to as an insight. It comes to consciousness suddenly, thus giving rise to the familiar Aha! moment. Such activation of remote associates naturally gives rise to comparisons to creativity, and the potential relationship between insight and creativity.

Insights are considered simply another way individuals produce creative solutions to problems. Neuroimaging studies suggest insights emanate predominantly from the right anterior superior temporal gyrus region of the brain, thus our understanding of the neural correlates involved in insight has increased considerably. It is generally accepted however, that creativity cannot be localized to a single region of the brain. Creativity appears to be highly lateralized in that several regions of the brain are active simultaneously. This makes sense, creativity involves many cognitive abilities, each of which involve many regions of the brain. Thus, creativity is not a moment of insight; however, insight can produce creativity if creativity happens to be the desired output [27]. In addition, it is worth noting that while the weak activation of a broad semantic field involved in insight is thought to be localized to the right hemisphere, thus perhaps giving rise to the popular myth that creative individuals are right-brained, there is no evidence to support such distinct brain lateralization, both hemispheres are active and contribute equally to creative problem solving.

Author details

Wesley Carpenter
The University of Akron, Akron, Ohio, USA

*Address all correspondence to: wac1@uakron.edu

References

[1] Kaplan CA, Simon HA. In search of insight. Cognitive Psychology. 1990;**22**:374-419

[2] Aziz-Zadeh L, Kaplan JT, Iacoboni M. "Aha!": The neural correlates of verbal insight solutions. Human Brain Mapping. 2009;**30**:908-916

[3] Schilpp PA. Albert Einstein: Autobiographical Notes (Centennial). Chicago: Open Court; 1979

[4] Jung-Beeman M, Bowden EM, Haberman J, Frymiare JL, Arambel-Liu S, et al. Neural activity when people solve verbal problems with insight. PLoS Biology. 2004;**2**(4):97

[5] Kounios J, Frymiare J, Bowden E, Fleck J, Subramaniam K, Parrish T, et al. The prepared mind: Neural activity prior to problem presentation predicts subsequent solution by sudden insight. Psychological Science. 2006;**17**:882-891. DOI: 10.1111/j.1467-9280.2006.01798.x

[6] Subramaniam K, Kounios J, Parrish TB, Jung-Beeman M. A brain mechanism for facilitation of insight by positive affect. Journal of Cognitive Neuroscience. 2009;**21**:415-432

[7] Kounios J, Fleck JI, Green DL, Payne L, Stevenson JL. The origins of insight in resting-state brain activity. Neuropsychologia. 2008;**46**(1):281-291

[8] Salvi C, Bricolo E, Kounios J, Bowden E, Beeman M. Insight solutions are correct more often than analytic solutions. Thinking and Reasoning. 2016;**22**(4):443-460. DOI: 10.1080/13546783.2016.1141798

[9] Bowden EM, Jung-Beeman M. Aha! Insight experience correlates with solution activation in the right hemisphere. Psychonomic Bulletin and Review. 2003;**10**(3):730-737. DOI: 10.3758/bf03196539

[10] Trope Y, Liberman N. Construal-level theory of psychological distance. Psychological Review. 2010;**117**:440-463

[11] Forster J, Friedman RS, Liberman N. Temporal construal effects on abstract and concrete thinking: Consequences for insight and creative cognition. Journal of Personality and Social Psychology. 2004;**87**:177-189

[12] Sheth BR, Sandkuhler S, Bhattacharya J. Posterior beta and anterior gamma oscillations predict cognitive insight. Journal Cognitive Neuroscience. 2008;**21**:1269-1279

[13] Kounios J, Beeman M. The Aha! moment: The cognitive neuroscience of insight. Current Directions in Psychological Science. 2009;**18**(4):210-216. DOI: 10.1111/j.1467-8721.2009.01638.x

[14] St George M, Kutas M, Martinez A, Sereno MI. Semantic integration in reading: Engagement of the right hemisphere during discourse processing. Brain. 1999;**122**:1317-1325

[15] Tallon-Baudry C, Bertrand O. Oscillatory gamma activity in humans and its role in object representation. Trends in Cognitive Science. 1999;**3**:151-162

[16] Sternberg RJ, Davidson J. The Nature of Insight. Cambridge, MA: MIT Press; 1995

[17] James W. Great Men, Great Thoughts, and the Environment (Lecture Delivered Before the Harvard Natural History Society). Boston, MA: Atlantic Monthly; 1880

[18] Dietrich A, Kanso R. A review of EEG, ERP, and neuroimaging studies of creativity and insight. Psychological Bulletin. 2010;**136**(5):822-848. DOI: 10.1037/A0019749

[19] Kohler W. The Mentality of Apes. London: Routledge & Kegan Paul; 1925

[20] Kohler W. The Task of Gestalt Psychology. Princeton, NJ: Princeton University Press; 1969

[21] MacGregor JN, Ormerod TC, Chronicle EP. Information processing and insight: A process model of performance on the nine-dot and related problems. Journal of Experimental Psychology: Learning, Memory, and Cognition. 2001;**27**:176-201

[22] Bowden EM, Jung-Beeman M, Fleck J, Kounios J. New approaches to demystifying insight. Trends in Cognitive Sciences. 2005;**9**(7):322-328. DOI: 10.1016/J.TICS.2005.05.012

[23] Sprugnoli G, Rossi S, Emmendorfer A, Rossi A, Liew S-L, Tatti E, et al. Neural correlates of Eureka moment. Intelligence. 2017;**62**:99-118

[24] Knoblich G, Ohlsson S, Haider H, Rhenius D. Constraint relaxation and chunk decomposition in insight problem solving. Journal of Experimental Psychology: Learning, Memory, and Cognition. 1999;**25**:1534-1555

[25] Jones G. Testing two cognitive theories of insight. Journal of Experimental Psychology: Learning, Memory, and Cognition. 2003;**29**(5):1017-1027. DOI: 10.1037/0278-7393.29.5.1017

[26] Knoblich G, Ohlsson S, Raney GE. An eye movement study of insight problem solving. Memory and Cognition. 2001;**29**:1000-1009

[27] Sawyer K. The cognitive neuroscience of creativity: A critical review. Creativity Research Journal. 2011;**23**(2):137-154. DOI: 10.1080/10400419.2011.571191

[28] Wallas G. The Art of Thought. New York: Harcourt Brace; 1926

[29] Runco MA. Creativity: Theories and Themes: Research, Development, and Practice. San Diego, CA: Academic Press; 2015

[30] Weisberg RW. Creativity: Genius and Other Myths. New York: W. H. Freeman; 1986

[31] Bowers KS, Farvolden P, Mermigis L. Intuitive antecedents of insight. In: Smith SM, Ward TB, Finke RA, editors. The Creative Cognition Approach. Cambridge, MA: MIT Press; 1995. pp. 27-51

[32] Hadamard J. The Psychology of Invention in the Mathematical Field. Princeton, NJ: Princeton University Press; 1945

[33] Ellwood S, Pallier G, Snyder A, Gallate J. The incubation effect: Hatching a solution? Creativity Research Journal. 2009;**21**:6-14

[34] Kohn N, Smith SM. Partly versus completely out of your mind: Effects of incubation and distraction on resolving fixation. Journal of Creative Behavior. 2009;**43**:102-118

[35] Patrick AS. The role of ability in creative "incubation.". Personality and Individual Differences. 1986;**7**(2):169-174

[36] Weisberg RW. Creativity: Beyond the Myth of Genius. New York: W. H. Freeman; 1993

[37] Schooler JW, Melcher J. The ineffability of insight. In: Smith SM, Ward TB, Finke RA, editors. The Creative Cognition Approach. Cambridge, MA: The MIT Press; 1995. pp. 97-133

[38] Kounios J, Beeman M. The cognitive neuroscience of insight. Annual Review of Psychology. 2014;**65**(1):71-93. DOI: 10.1146/annurev-psych-010213-115154

[39] Mumford MD, Whetzel DL. Insight, creativity, and cognition: On Sternberg and Davidson's the nature of insight. Creativity Research Journal. 1996;**9**(1):103-107

[40] Mednick SA. The associative basis of the creative process. Psychological Review. 1962;**69**:220-232

Chapter 3

Crowdsourcing in the Fashion Industry

Luigi Nasta and Luca Pirolo

Abstract

In today's cutthroat competitive world of fashion, flexibility and adaptability are essential elements for a company to survive in this industry. As such, there is a growing interest for open innovation and crowdsourcing as tools that might boost the competitiveness in the industry. By embracing open innovation, the use of external knowledge to emphasize internal creativity and expand market influence, industries can reach beyond their own internal resources and develop better ideas, faster and at a lower cost. The fashion industry is no exception. Specifically, crowdsourcing is lowering the fashion industry's barriers to entry and giving the public an opportunity to not just shape a brand but also determine the trends of an entire sector. This chapter aims at analyzing the features, the pros, and the cons of crowdsourcing in the fashion industry focusing on the perspectives of both the companies and the customers.

Keywords: crowdsourcing, open innovation, co-creation, fashion industry, business model innovation

1. Crowdsourcing: from its origins to the recent implementations in the fashion industry

At a first glance, crowdsourcing is a relatively new concept in (and not only) the management studies. Actually, Howe [1] traced the very first example of crowdsourcing to 1714, when the British government announced a competition on the idea of a way to establish the longitude of a sailing ship during navigation, offering a reward of 20,000 pounds to anyone who managed to find a solution. The Royal Navy and the greatest scientists, among them Isaac Newton, had failed in trying to develop a tool capable of calculating longitude and it was a cabinetmaker named John Harrison to devise a watch able to find this measurement with great precision even during trips to the open sea. Thus, a subject who had not received any specific training in the field won the award by designing the first model of marine chronometer, an effective solution to the problem of the British government, reached by submitting it to an extremely broad public and with the most varied skills.

From an etymological point of view, the term "crowdsourcing" was coined by Jeff Howe in an article entitled The Rise of Crowdsourcing and published in the Wired magazine in the June 2006 edition. Howe combines the words "crowd," i.e., crowd/common people, and "sourcing," intended as assignment or procurement, to describe the act performed by a company or an institution consisting in outsourcing an activity, normally carried out by its members, to a network of people not linked by organizational constraints and usually strangers to each other.

The two macro-phenomena that led to the birth of crowdsourcing according to Pellegrini [2] are the crisis of the industrial economic system, which has stimulated the search for new ways of finding and organizing resources and creating value, whose primary source has become knowledge, and the incessant development of networks that allow the connection and communication between people more or less close to each other, primarily of the Web. About the Web, the most significant evolutionary step of the Internet is that from Web 1.0 to Web 2.0, which is traced back to 2004, when the American publisher O'Reilly Media organized a series of conferences on new user network opportunities. While the Web 1.0 made it possible to simply browse through the pages of static sites and without interaction methods, or the only acquisition and dissemination of encoded knowledge (information), Web 2.0 is characterized by the interactive aspect, which allows user no longer just to enjoy, but also to create content. Today, therefore, the Internet allows us to enhance human intelligence, provides a means for the creation of new knowledge, considering the difficulty and inadequacy of codification in environmental complexity, and encourages sharing and participation in projects and innovations. Moreover, the development of the Web, as a production tool free from logistic constraints, has contributed to creating a growing number of intangible assets, further increasing the value attributed to knowledge.

Therefore, crowdsourcing is a product of the knowledge society. As described by Pellegrini [2], the knowledge economy is characterized by the search for forms of collaboration and sharing to strength the ability of interpretation and action of organizations in a highly dynamic reference environment, and by the desire of consumers to assume a growing awareness and to become an active part of the creative and productive processes.

Considering a more micro level of analysis, and therefore evaluating in detail the origins of crowdsourcing, the main phenomena that have prepared fertile ground and influenced its development are the activities of innovation and user customization. These phenomena are attributable to the logic of prosumerism and to the movement of open source software, to which are added, feeding them, the democratization of information, of the means of production and distribution and the evolution of networks and of online communities.

These trends seem to affect every economic sector in a huge number of industries. Nevertheless, the most significant and fruitful implications are coming out from those industries where the active involvement of external stakeholders in the decision-making processes, during the ideation and all prior stages of the production activity, can generate a meaningful and substantial reduction in cost function and risk management. To achieve this efficiency goal, among all firm's stakeholders, a special focus has to be addressed toward customers. Transforming current and potential customers from mere buyers to actors with a voice in the firm's decisions is a strategic way to motivate them and build a bond of trust sustainable over time.

For a long period of time, the textile industry, the apparel industry, and the accessories industry, or—more in general—the fashion world, have based their businesses on the ability to predict (and in the same case to impose) what people wanted [3]. Marketing departments, as well as style and creative directions acting in the main fashion companies, are characterized for a huge apparatus for selecting what is going to be popular in the next future. Based on these expectations, they create new collections available in the market. Nonetheless, the democratization process that worldwide is affecting every industry has recently occurred also in the fashion system, where potentially anyone could be a designer, a creator, or a manufacturer. Moreover, the symbolic value attributed to fashion products calls for a more active role of the customer, which becomes part of the key successful factors on which the brand equity has to be built.

1.1 Prosumerism, user innovation, and customization

The profound awareness of one's own needs and the tendency to privilege the symbolic meaning of goods as an expression of one's own identity have increasingly encouraged consumers of the knowledge society to manipulate the outputs of enterprises, both on the semantic level, through the attribution of meaning, and on the one related to tangible characteristics and components, giving life to the idea of prosumerism [4]. Some subjects, that for their particular and innovative skills take the name of "lead user", have come to develop into solutions that meet their needs and, in some industrial sectors, are even the architects of most new products and services [5]. The innovations created by users, defined "user driven innovation" (or simply "user innovation"), include changes made directly to the goods produced by a company, proposals for changes in design and/or in properties submitted to an organization, and products created in a complete and personal way.

Seizing this trend, some companies, Nike and Levi's among the first, decided to involve customers in their creative activities on their own initiative, allowing them to customize standard articles through a platform on the company Website [6, 7]. This first step taken by organizations toward the possibility of voluntarily involving consumers in production cycles is described as "mass customization" and consists of the attempt to combine mass production with customization, maintaining cost efficiency and developing greater flexibility and ability to meet the specific needs of individuals. One aspect of the customization activity performed by customers, that is particularly significant and apparently paradoxical, is its free nature, considerable as an emblem of the main motivation that pushes consumers to do their job, that is the satisfaction obtainable through the subsequent consumption of the personalized product and often also through the creative action itself.

Over time, the collaboration of companies with users has intensified, in particular addressing the co-creation of new offers together with the lead users, which are in fact recognized of the features that can be advantageously exploited in the problem-solving processes of the organizations and above all in innovation projects. Specifically, Von Hippel [8] identified two distinctive elements of these consumers: the ability to predict market trends, experiencing first of the needs that will emerge in the future in the entire population of which they are part, and the great motivation to identify a solution that satisfies them, determined by the high benefit they can derive from it. These two aspects are strongly correlated with the likelihood that lead users to engage in the development of new products or in the modification of existing ones, further increased by their significant degree of expertise. As a result, as it has been demonstrated by several studies, most of the user innovations are carried out by subjects belonging to the category of lead users, and even the attractiveness they exert toward the companies and the intention of the latter to translate them into commercial products increase proportionally compared to the extent to which the designers have this connotation. These dynamics are the prelude to open innovation, of which crowdsourcing is sometimes defined as one of the key techniques [9], and which in any case provides many collaborative ideas and development elements to this model of joint problem solving.

In close connection with the ambition of consumers to become producers, the phenomenon of amateurs has arisen, who realize by passion and without receiving a form of income the same tasks that other specialized subjects perform by profession. The amateur rebirth, which stimulates, among other things, the collaboration between people with professional backgrounds and very different skills, is defined by Howe [1] as "the fuel for the crowdsourcing engine."

One factor that has greatly influenced the rise of amateur activities, and consequently also the development of crowdsourcing, is the search for rewarding experiences outside the work environment, prompted in turn by the high rate of job dissatisfaction, caused by demand from the world of work of ever greater levels of specialization and the resulting impossibility of many individuals to feel fulfilled, despite the quality of their training and the variety of interests and knowledge.

Thanks to the increasing degree of education of the company, to the ease of access to information, favored by the dissemination of news and knowledge through the Web, and to a sort of democratization of the production instruments, extremely cheaper and easier to use, the heritage of knowledge and skills, that both consumers and amateurs are in possession of, is increasingly richer and allows them to compete with professionals substantially in all fields of knowledge (information technology, journalism, science, etc.). This leads to the emergence of the figure of the prosumer and that of the Pro-Am, identified by Charles Leadbeater and Paul Miller [10] and resumed by Howe [1], which shares the quantity and quality of the commitment lavished by the amateur, such as to compare it to professional work. The appearance and the emergence of these subjects have certainly played an important role in the development of crowdsourcing, but the people that make up the crowd, and to which the organizations can therefore turn for a collaborative problem-solving action, not necessarily can be qualified as prosumers and Pro-Am according to their precise definition. In fact, crowdsourcing can involve individuals potentially endowed with any degree of specialization and professionalism (experts in the field, scientists of the discipline, fans of the subject, consumers of the product, etc.), but generally united by the desire to participate and lend their own work in a specific project mainly not for an economic return but for reasons related to pleasure, interest, leisure, and personal satisfaction. Crowdsourcing can provide for forms of material compensation, i.e., prizes and rewards of various entities, which can encourage participation, but these do not prevail over amateur reasons.

1.2 Open innovation and crowdsourcing

Another influential phenomenon on crowdsourcing is open innovation. Specifically, open innovation emerges from the extension of the collaborative approach of an organization with consumers, and in particular with lead users, to a wider variety of partners, also welcoming the ideas of wisdom of crowd and transparency that can be found in the open source model. The concept was introduced for the first time by Henry Chesbrough, the author of the book Open Innovation: The New Imperative for Creating and Profiting from Technology [11], and is based in particular on the need for an organization to open up to cooperation with external actors at its own boundaries in research and development activities, to obtain technological and above all cognitive resources, taking up the key points of the approach of collaborative networks regarding interorganizational relations, but naturally referring to all the possible relations of the company with external subjects. In fact, open innovation is also born as an answer to the environmental uncertainty, to the complexity of innovative processes, and to the increasing diffusion of knowledge in society and is realized in a growing degree of permeability of organizational boundaries and in the connected adoption of more open interaction methods with an ever-wider range of stakeholders, including consumers, suppliers, competitors, and universities [12–14]. Chesbrough [15] underlined the need to overcome the closed innovation approach, especially in sectors such as information technology, where the life cycle of products is very short, and it is not possible to exercise sufficient control over the dynamics of the market. In particular, in these circumstances, it would be more effective to increase transparency and to share resources and opportunities among the actors present in the environment.

Gassmann and Enkel [16] identified three possible models of open innovation: the outside-in model, which favors an enrichment of the skills of a company, thanks to the integration of external sources of knowledge in the processes of knowledge creation; the model inside-out, which involves an inverse process, i.e., the outsourcing of internally generated ideas and innovations making them available for exploitation by other subjects in the reference environment, an alliance model between different partners that consists of a combination of the two previous approaches. How the logic of open innovation is implemented includes contestations and competitions of various kinds, alliances, joint ventures, licensing agreements, open source platforms, and development communities [14].

Seltzer and Mahmoudi [9], considering the natural dependence of the effectiveness of open innovation processes from the contributions of external actors in terms of innovative ideas and new knowledge for an organization, listed a series of management and implementation practices. First and foremost, an open company should attract a large group of collaborators, grasping the teaching of open source experiences, define the expectations on the level of partner participation, and identify ways to profit from open innovation, balancing the aspects of creation and appropriation of value through a real open strategy. As for the implementation methods, the company can decide, for example, to draw up a contract of various types with competitors or not, to commission the development of ideas to key customers, to create partnerships with suppliers, and to resort to crowdsourcing.

Therefore, crowdsourcing can be seen as a strategy of implementing open innovation, but, according to another possible perspective, also as an independent problem-solving technique that intersects with the practice of open innovation if the problems faced are linked precisely to innovative processes. However, the distinction between these interpretations tends to fade if one examines the meaning attributed to the term "innovation", as a creative and efficient recombination of existing inputs to produce new value outputs [14], substantially coinciding with the current conception of an effective problem-solving activity.

In any case, crowdsourcing finds both the need for an organization to open up to the flow of external knowledge as well as the idea of creating the value of the philosophy of open innovation as integration and transformation of internal and external resources and skills. Consequently, in addition to the management techniques introduced a little above, there are several measures that can be implemented for open innovation activities that can also be validly used in the organization of crowdsourcing. These include an accurate description of the problem to be solved, without revealing the possible solution options developed by the organization, so as not to influence and therefore fully exploit the thinking and the potential for reflection of the subjects involved from the outside; a careful definition of the context in which the problem is placed, so that the issue to be addressed is clear; a complete illustration of the concepts, without taking their knowledge for granted; the exposure of the limits of the company in applying a possible solution, so as to limit the research to the feasible options; sharing all available knowledge; and finally an orientation toward quality results that, even under different aspects, have a value for all the people involved in the innovation process [17].

2. Structure and declinations of crowdsourcing

Zhao and Zhu [18] defined crowdsourcing as a "collective intelligence system" and identified three constituent components of the model, i.e. the crowd, the organization that uses this problem-solving mode and therefore benefits from the work of the crowd, called client company, and the place, physical or virtual, which allows the connection between these two protagonists and hosts all the activities of the process.

Considering the various categories, we can see the flexible nature of crowdsourcing, which can in fact take many activities into its logic, revealing a model that can be applied in a variety of situations and even not only in the economic but also scientific, political, social, and many other sectors. Brabham [19] noted that crowdsourcing, with the diversity of its possible applications in a plurality of industries, stands as a model for solving both daily and rather trivial and complex problems. Furthermore, he argues that it is not merely an approach to the exploitation of reports and contributions enabled by the Web, but a real strategic model aimed at attracting a large group of individuals interested, motivated, and able to develop solutions superior to those achievable through the most traditional forms of business and procedures, both from a quantitative and a qualitative point of view.

From this conceptual perspective, crowdsourcing is experiencing a clear success in the fashion system. In fact, this phenomenon is significantly modifying the structure of the industry from both a productive and retailing points of views. Indeed, the number of firms diving into the crowdsourcing arena is growing exponentially and examples include every step of the value chain.

For the purpose of mapping the strategies and the main outcomes of the crowdsourcing activities, we propose to investigate them according to the stage of a fashion firm's production cycle in which it can occur. Ideally, following a traditional fashion value chain, we can identify four main phases: inspiration, creation, production, and distribution [20].

Traditionally, the inspiration phase is a matter of the designers of the fashion firms: they usually conduct a personal analysis of new trends and market preferences to develop the concept of the new collection. The ability to identify and catch the right stimuli is the real foundation for the success of this stage. Starting from this consideration, the involvement of the customer base is a good means to monitor their preferences and develop new ideas consistent with them. Many firms regularly use polls, focus group or man-on-the-street observations and interviews to track any changes in tastes and trends, but crowdsourcing offers a reach and a dialog on a wider scale unreachable with other traditional marketing techniques.

The second phase—the creation—starts with the approval by the firm's creative direction of the collection concept and it consists of the realization of the first prototypes. In other words, this is the product design step where a set of strategic and operational activities turns ideas into tangible products. Here, again we can underline the same considerations about the value that a crowdsourcing technique can bring in coping with the risks.

With the third phase, the firm launches the production, supporting ex ante all costs. In fact, fashion companies try to create value by producing clothes that people want to wear and bearing the connected economic and financial risks. In order to reduce these risks, firms can conduct product test on some items, but the results of this activity can be hardly generalized to the entire collection and to all available markets.

Finally, with the distribution phase, firms plan their placement and strategies leveraging on market tests conducted on the most significant geographical areas.

This pattern is consistent with the four possible variations of crowdsourcing proposed in the literature and described below. Specifically, we want to identify under which conditions the four possible configurations of crowdsourcing can match with the different phase of the production cycles previously described, without highlighting any single and exclusive link between each step of the value chain and each crowdsourcing configuration.

2.1 Crowd wisdom

The first of the forms of crowdsourcing listed is based entirely on crowd wisdom, fully sharing its principles, so much to be identified with it. The choice to resort to this type therefore stems from the desire to exploit the knowledge of a large number of people, recognizing the egalitarian hypothesis expressed by Howe [1], so each individual has some knowledge or talent that is of value for some other individual. The goal of crowdsourcing is therefore to connect those who hold a knowledge with those who consider it useful and, since everyone can provide some valuable contributions to the level of knowledge, thanks to their private information, to extend as much as possible this network of connections.

A fundamental concept that supports the search for the involvement of a multitude of subjects in decision-making processes is the one formulated by the "Theorem of diversity that beats talent", interpreted in the book by Ostrom [21] "The Difference. How the Power of Diversity creates Better Groups, Enterprises, Schools and Societies", which proposes a logical/mathematical analysis of collective intelligence. Along this conceptual framework, Page [22] stated that, given certain circumstances, the solutions developed by a randomly selected group of people are seen by a group of selected subjects as the best results. This theorem, verified by many academic studies [23], is based on the observation that the talented subjects, in a given field, constitute a homogeneous group, since, in most cases, they have followed the same training path, even attending the same schools, and consequently, they tend to apply similar, if not identical, solutions to processes and problems. Specialized knowledge is better than generic knowledge, but in its specific context of reference and, moreover, the resolution of most problems, especially of those that are complex, implies the appeal to different spheres of knowledge.

Therefore, the experts are better than the crowd, but in less contexts, and the latter generally obtains the most effective results in the problem-solving processes, being able to count on a wide variety of heuristics and solution techniques.

Page's theorem affirms the essence of collective intelligence, that is, the belief that the combined action of a group of different people can lead to a better decision than any person individually could take. This principle directly links another significant aspect that can be found in problem-solving activities, namely the high probability that solutions emerge from the most unexpected subjects. According to Lakhani et al. [24], this counter-intuitive outcome derives from the ability of the actors who are intellectually distant from the field of skills that would tend to apply to a given problem to interpret the question in a new way, according to different perspectives, and to apply solutions that are known to them but unusual in that domain of knowledge. The so-called breakthrough thinking emerges almost always in subjects who have not had previous experience in the area in which the problem is inserted, precisely because they are free of conditioning and conjectures on the techniques considered traditionally suitable for the resolutive approach. Applying the theory of diversity, crowdsourcing favors this result, since it involves a group of people endowed with skills in different fields and therefore analyzes the situation to be faced according to alternative and often unusual perspectives.

Howe [1] realized that a company that decides to rely on crowd wisdom to find the solution to its problem outperforms the predominant trend in business (and also in human networks) to address people and other similar organizations, which, since they are similar, they know each other well and consequently adopt similar methods of analysis and action. In this case, crowdsourcing makes use of the "strength of weak bonds", as defined by sociologists, i.e., the greater possibility of progress provided by unknown actors and realities, which bring new ideas and new approaches to resolution, which on the one hand, thanks to their variety, increase the probability of finding a solution and on the other could also determine the discovery of an unexpected line of action which proves to be superior to the options drawn by the traditional heuristics.

Today, companies exploit collective intelligence in problem-solving processes, anticipating future results and addressing company strategies. In particular, Howe [1] indicated for crowd wisdom based crowdsourcing three even more specific connotations, namely the application in the market of forecasts (or information market), the crowdcasting, which consists in the assignment of a business problem to a network indefinite of potential external solvers, and the idea jam (or idea dump, translatable as "crowd of ideas"), which aims to gather many ideas and insights into a brainstorming logic, without reference to a specific problem to be addressed. In the case of the forecast market, the crowd is assigned the task of predicting the winner of some kind of competition or the result to which a certain "future" contract is linked. In crowdcasting, the actors involved in the network can decide to tackle problem-solving activities individually or to organize themselves in groups. Finally, the idea jam usually envisages the development of crowdsourcing on the Web, configuring itself as a sort of online suggestion box and allowing anyone to propose their own ideas, which can then be discussed with other people.

In general, in this first analyzed form of crowdsourcing, discussions and the search for a consensus among the actors involved in the process are avoided, as the strength of this model lies in the sum of the differences, which are maintained by leaving each his own autonomy, while aggregating the contributions of all, so many separate actions are realized that flow into a collective problem-solving activity.

Moving on to the debate on our field, the wisdom configuration of crowdsourcing allows fashion companies to aggregate the knowledge of a large number of current and potential new customers in exploiting new trends and tastes in the fashion industry.

Evidence shows numerous examples of the benefits of this activity. A very interesting case comes from Nike. Back in 1999, the sportswear firm introduced customized sneakers and currently it has broadened the program including a huge variety of options also on clothing and sport equipment until to let customers to share and order each other's design in its online gallery as well as in its app developed for Android and Apple users. The most recent development in improving Nike's customer shopping experience is the "Consumer Direct Offense", a new company alignment that allows Nike to better serve the consumer personally, at scale. In the new alignment, the company drives growth by deeply serving consumers through personalized services in 12 key cities, across 10 key countries: New York, London, Shanghai, Beijing, Los Angeles, Tokyo, Paris, Berlin, Mexico City, Barcelona, Seoul, and Milan. These key cities and countries are expected to represent over 80% of Nike's projected growth through 2020.

Moreover, stressing on the problem-solving final aim, usually associated with the crowd wisdom, this configuration of crowdsourcing can support fashion firms in identifying solutions to specific managerial issues. An example is represented by the "Design the next Coach Tote" campaign launched by Coach to engage a younger market, both ensuring the successful understanding of its customers' needs and repositioning its brand on this segment of the market. The campaign, conceived to allow consumers to design their own Coach bag, was successful, thanks to more than 1700 participants and 3200 submissions of new different tote bag designs over 6 weeks. Currently, the company still offers the possibility to personalize some bags and sneakers with the choice of patterns and pins.

2.2 Crowd creation

The second declination of crowdsourcing described by Howe [1] is aimed at exploiting the creative energies of the crowd, which translate into user generated content, or online content, innovative ideas, and new products, made in a collaborative way. The desire of the companies that make use of this form of crowdsourcing is precisely that of channeling the creativity of the external stakeholders in their commercial offer, through the creation of a community production.

The processes of crowd creation differ greatly from those that use collective intelligence, based on the interaction between the subjects involved in a given work, which is instead avoided by crowd wisdom in order to protect the diversity of thought. The aggregation of dispersed know-how developed autonomously is thus replaced by the formation or support of a community of individuals who share the passion for a certain activity and who, driven by the affinity descending from this common interest, want to confront and communicate with each other. Therefore, the fundamental element that makes crowd creation possible is the social environment, and the protagonists of this type of crowdsourcing are the communities that emerge, mostly spontaneously, in the new ecosystem of interconnected subjects.

The central role assigned to communities highlights another fundamental difference between crowd creation and the exploitation of crowd wisdom: while the decision of a company to make use of collective intelligence appears to be an alternative to other problem-solving techniques, by offering new but in any case, additive value with respect to internal tools and resources, the involvement of communities formed autonomously by amateurs and consumers is sometimes an almost obligatory choice. In fact, these communities constantly increase their capacity to perform functions similar to those of companies, with the risk of threatening the survival of the latter, if they are not able to recognize and benefit from the increased skills and organization of their stakeholders. Moreover, since communities formed by amateurs and/or consumers self-organize, they do not allow themselves to be managed, but can only be guided by companies. Therefore, it is not easy for an organization to be able to build and maintain these groups, toward and in which full transparency must be guaranteed, in such a way that a relationship of trust and real partnership between company and crowd is created. In fact, the latter must not feel exploited, but must perceive a balance between the advantages offered and received through the work of the crowdsourced work, which leads to the achievement of effective and efficient results precisely in conditions of harmony between the company and the community. The self-organization of the communities is itself one of the main sources of efficiency of crowd creation, as it substantially corresponds to their ability to distribute intellectual resources in an organic way, which is more functional to problem-solving processes than a hierarchical structure of tasks and knowledge.

The development of this second form of crowdsourcing takes place through the interactions of the members of a community, who actually act collaboratively, assisting each other and exchanging opinions. Because of the benefit directly obtainable from the solution and/or from the job, these subjects are strongly motivated to participate in the problem-solving process, normally linked to the commercial offer of the company, and to favor the achievement of the best possible result. Consequently, crowd creation activities are characterized by the search for an improvement of their knowledge and skills and, therefore, by the predominant role of learning processes.

The user generated content, with which we normally refer to as the content produced and published on the Web by consumers, is one of the main forms of crowd creation, which often takes place via an online platform. In fact, users have increasingly revealed the desire not only to take part in the creative and productive activities of companies, but also to interact with the media, synergistically combining these two aspects and providing their contributions via the Internet. The latter, thanks above all to the more interactive connotation of Web 2.0, lends itself to a cooperative approach to work, naturally encouraging the exchange of information and ideas and a decentralized but almost unlimited participation. However, by accepting a smaller presence of subjects involved, this type of crowdsourcing can take place profitably even in a physical place, which may represent a better choice than the online environment depending, for example, on the level of complexity of the problem to be addressed or on the degree and type of interactions required for the dissemination and creation of knowledge.

Among the several examples of the application of crowd creation in the fashion industry, some interesting cases emerge from the footwear sector. In fact, as the Nike example previously described shows, the footwear industry seems to be one of the most vibrant sectors in the fashion industry, as previous studies underlined [25–27]. Among the most dynamic firms, Keds is perhaps the largest and best-known company whose success is based on its ability to set up a marketplace for customized products. Launched in 2008, the "Keds design your own custom shoes" program lets on line customers to choose among a huge selection of alternatives to personalize their own sneakers. Moreover, for a period of time, visitors could share and sell their creations on Zazzle.com, setting their own royalty from 10 to 99% above the base shoe price of $60. Furthermore, Keds, together with the American department store chain Bloomingdale's and the Whitney Museum, has created a project to sell art to the masses in the form of footwear. Acting as sponsor of the Whitney Museum of American Art Summer Season, Keds launched the KedsWhitney shoe collection, consisting of sneakers designed by conceptual artist Jenny Holzer, who created limited-edition shoes sold at Bloomingdale's stores in Midtown and SoHo.

2.3 Crowd voting

The third form of crowdsourcing aimed at exploiting the skills of the crowd arises essentially from the difficulty for a company to evaluate all the numerous contributions that the crowd itself provides in the context of a given activity entrusted to it. The complexity of analysis evidently increases proportionally to the quantity of ideas and solutions proposed and, therefore, the use of crowd voting is mainly found after problem-solving processes based on crowd wisdom or idea jam sessions. To overcome the problem of examining the multiplicity and diversity of contributions, the power to judge them is shifted from producers to consumers, so "the crowd provides creative talent as well as acumen to evaluate this talent" [1].

These filtering operations of proposals and decision between them can easily take place online and are even the preferred tool for the governance and classification of information on the Web, which no single individual or company could be able to organize. In fact, the Google search engine, recognizing the possibility of ordering an immense amount of information and notions through the aggregation of individual decisions, attributes to Internet users the power to determine the value of information, which moreover is exercised without any additional effort, through normal browsing behavior. However, online voting also presents a risk of alteration of the results through vote buying and selling actions, which clearly compromise the validity of the overall judgment.

The collective choices resulting from crowd voting are therefore a collaborative filter, which allows organizing information and contributions based on the relevance that is attributed to them. This result is achieved both in the case in which the judging mechanism is passive (as is the case with Google) and in the case in which it is active. The passive filter is configured as a sort of unconscious evaluation, using the data generated by the choices and the digital paths of the various users of the network as a database of organizational knowledge, to be exploited in the management and classification of information. The active filter, on the other hand, coincides with a form of analysis and conscious decision by people, who are explicitly called to express their judgment on a set of contributions.

Companies that decide to implement a form of crowd voting learn opinions and needs of consumers, which allow, for example, a better understanding of the demand for products and services offered and to schedule production accordingly; they also promote consensus and trust stakeholders who want to be involved in business processes.

With particular reference to participatory media, Howe [1] reported a rule that summarizes the dynamics of the first three declinations of crowdsourcing from the point of view of participation, the value and the type of contribution made by the subjects that make up the crowd: the "rule 1:10:89," according to which "of every one hundred people on a given site, one will really create something, 10 will vote for what it has created and the remaining 89 will simply consume creation." Ten percent, by examining and evaluating ideas, actually performs an activity that is just as important as that of making contributions, so much so that it can still be considered a mode of creation.

Crowd voting in the fashion industry can be used according to two different patterns: firms can adopt a selective or a collective approach, depending on the role they let their customers play.

In the selective form, fashion firms seek for new ideas coming from the public and then choose how many and which among the proposed options drive into mass production. To achieve this result, companies can launch a specific contest, addressed to current and potential customers, to collect ideas for new product developments through software available online or via an app. In turn, the selection process can be guided by internal or external decision-making mechanisms. The internal selection is usually based on the verification of the matching between the characteristics of the products proposed by customers and the heritage values of the firms as well as its positioning in the market. Instead, the external selection is entrusted to a public voting, giving the customers a say in the choosing and buying process of a fashion firm. Examples of the selective crowdsourcing are the campaign "Design the next Coach Tote", previously described, or the website Threadless.

Threadless is an e-commerce, created in 2000, and founded on an online community of artists and potential buyers who create and chose the items to be sold on the website. Each week, about 1000 designs are submitted online and are put to a public vote. Threadless allows users to vote on designs and rate them on a scale from 1 to 5. Designs are scored by the community for 1 week, before being reviewed by the Threadless staff. Based on the average score and community feedback, about 10 designs are selected each week, printed on clothing and other products, and sold worldwide through the online store and at their retail store in Chicago.

2.4 Crowdfunding

While the first three configurations of crowdsourcing enhance the skills of a crowd, in particular the knowledge and creative skills, the fourth one considers the crowd as a source of financial resources. In fact, crowdfunding, also known as "social banking", presents some peculiarities that make it a form in a certain sense comparable to the others. In fact, crowdfunding does not exploit the skills and creativity of the stakeholders, or their judgments, but their economic availability. However, Howe [1] highlighted a series of typical aspects of crowdsourcing that are also found in this type, namely the radical change induced in the organization of a sector, the removal of hierarchies, and the direct link between those who hold a resource and who needs it, the democratic impulse.

In addition to the direct benefit of obtaining funds, crowdfunding allows you to know if anyone is specifically interested in the development of a certain project or product, as the will to contribute financially can only be dictated by sharing the objective to be achieved or the desire to be able to purchase and consume a new product/service, with certain characteristics and with a certain quality level. Therefore, considering this declination of crowdsourcing from the perspective of problem solving, the positive impact emerges on the creation of consensus and motivation, as well as on the ability to cope with any threats and to seize the opportunities that may arise in the transactional environment.

This last configuration of crowdsourcing is straightforward to be applied to any industry, including fashion. As shown by the various crowdfunding platforms for gathering money from the public, such as Kickstarter, this phenomenon is typical of new ventures with innovative ideas to be developed. Looking at the only fashion projects available on Kickstarter (more than 25,000), it is clear how much this configuration meets the interest of start-ups and investors, also thanks to the rules that govern the funding mechanism: project creators choose a deadline and a minimum funding goal. If the goal is not met by the deadline, no funds are collected.

3. Pros and cons of crowdsourcing

3.1 Advantages of crowdsourcing

Crowdsourcing, as outsourcing a business to the crowd, implies for the company the achievement of benefits linked to both costs and risks [28]. About the economic aspect, the company is basically free to define the amount of remuneration, which can be significantly reduced compared to that relating to a function performed in outsourcing, if not even nonexistent. In fact, although professionals can also lend their jobs as part of a crowdsourcing project, they are considered on the same level as most contributors, including amateurs, consumers, and individuals wishing to spend their free time or a period of unemployment exploiting their knowledge and skills and are therefore motivated above all by opportunities for personal satisfaction, an increase in social reputation, and the reporting of their skills. A form of compensation, however limited, should still be offered, due to the positive link with the degree of involvement of people in the problem-solving process, which, among other things, considers participation in crowdsourcing, and in particular that related to complex activities, as a source of additional income. In any case, the company that decides to monetarily reward the parties that provide their contribution is obliged to pay only if the results achieved meet its expectations. Moreover, if the participants in the crowdsourcing activity are consumers of the company's products, the latter has less need to monitor the feedback on the products and, consequently, the testing phases that follow that of research and development are simpler, faster, and naturally less expensive. In addition, by examining the effects of crowdsourcing on the risks borne by the company, on the one hand, the risk deriving from the dependence on a single supplier is substantially eliminated, and on the other hand, the risk of failure inherent in any process of problem solving is externalized, also considering that the possibility that the contributions obtained are not satisfactory is limited, thanks to a system of monetary incentives.

In addition to the cost and risk advantages, of course, the use of crowdsourcing can have a positive effect on the quality of the results achieved through the problem-solving processes. The literature, examining numerous cases of crowdsourcing, reveals how the factual outcomes of this model are better or good at least as much as those produced through other methods of problem solving [29]. Schenk and Guittard [30] highlighted the variety of impacts that the model exercises according to the type of outsourced activity, to which corresponds the same quality perception diversity. Indeed, when the crowd performs routine tasks for a company, the benefit for the latter in terms of quality depends on the access to a more or less large pool of contributions, with a more or less complementary nature. In the opposite situation of developing a complex project, quality refers to the characteristics of the elaborated solutions, also considering their different trade-offs and technological paths. Finally, the quality of creative activities coincides with the originality of the crowd's proposals that are assessed comparing them to the company's expectations.

On the other hand, it is more difficult to judge the impact of crowdsourcing on perceptual results; however, the empirical evidence and in particular the rapid increase in crowdsourcing projects and the growth of related expenses suggest a positive impact on the degree of satisfaction of the participants [29]. Moreover, the possibility of contributing to the company processes positively influences the trust and loyalty of the stakeholders toward the organization, since it stimulates their sense of belonging.

Performing a more detailed analysis, we can indicate a series of specific advantages of each of the crowdsourcing declinations identified by Howe [1]. In particular, the benefits offered by the exploitation of the crowd wisdom are linked to access to a wide range of knowledge and to the creation of linking networks between holders and researchers of skills. The crowd creation, in addition to providing a variety of creative ideas, is a valuable tool for the interaction between business and emerging communities in the current scenario dominated by interconnections and for the stimulation of processes for the dissemination of knowledge and constant learning. On the other hand, crowd voting, in the first place, considerably reduces the complexity of the decision-making process, with specific reference to the selection phase of the solution to be implemented, and, secondly, allows the company to find information on consumer preferences. Finally, crowdfunding makes it possible to overcome financial barriers that may hinder or even prevent the realization of a project and fosters both the knowledge of its stakeholders and the approval by them of the actions implemented by the organization.

In general, the incentives to adopt the crowdsourcing model and therefore the main advantages achievable are the availability of a highly motivated and committed workforce that lends itself to perform certain company functions at an extremely low cost for the company that outsources them, the ability to quickly execute large quantities of work and solve problems that are too long and/or complex to be dealt with by a single subject, and, given the benefits listed above, the opportunity to achieve better results overall than those obtainable through other business models and forms of collaboration.

Moreover, in an environment that asks organizations to continuously know how to evolve and adapt, requiring the priority development of dynamic skills and innovative processes, crowdsourcing can also be chosen as a means to foster creativity, both at the individual and at the organizational level, and the consequent innovation. In fact, crowdsourcing seems to facilitate the coexistence of the characteristics of successful innovators, emerged from the Root-Bernstein ten-year study [31]: a good command of knowledge and fundamental tools of the business sector, which is not the only field of specialization and combines with information and concepts belonging to other areas, curiosity and interest primarily for the problem and then for the solution, the attitude to question dominant models and hypotheses, and the conception of knowledge as an integrated form and the search for solutions of a global rather than particular nature. The members of the crowd each possess a unique heritage of knowledge, which can be more or less generic and variously exploitable in the activities outsourced by the client company, but certainly suitable for analyzing the problem according to original perspectives. In addition to the versatility inherent in the crowd, the company benefits from the strong interest of those involved in a crowdsourcing project for the problem faced, often deriving from the desire to involve in creative processes or the opportunity to put their skills at stake, increasing personal satisfaction and reputation, and, in these circumstances, pre-eminent to that for the solution. Finally, knowledge is now perceived by the crowd as social knowledge, an overall knowledge to which everyone can contribute and of which everyone can benefit, in a logic to which even businesses are called to approach.

3.2 Risks of crowdsourcing

The use of crowdsourcing also involves risks for a company, some common to the outsourcing model and others specific to this phenomenon. As in the case of outsourcing, an organization that assigns the crowd to carry out its activities can renounce moments of learning and the creation of new in-house skills [30]. However, this disadvantage can be limited by constant monitoring by the company of the problem-solving process carried out by the crowd, which is possible in cases of project development in a physical place, where both people who lend their own work can be present as well as the client company, or by preparing appropriate online monitoring tools.

A specific risk of crowdsourcing, and in particular of online forms, derives from the assignment of the organization to a platform owned by third parties and, consequently, from partial dependence on the strategic choices made by these, which at the same time can provide an important support in the management of the process. Another aspect to the detriment of this specific model of joint problem solving is linked to human costs and indeed consists of the negative effect on the subjects involved in terms of compensation for their work. In fact, despite the perceived fairness in the relationship between organization and crowd, which—as highlighted more times—obtains the greatest satisfaction from the activity itself and/or from the result of the same, and not through any monetary compensations, the performances executed have a value far superior in comparison to the remuneration offered for the winning solutions [19]. The amount of payments provided by the company is in no way proportionate to the high quality of the contributions received, which, if acquired through the classic labor market rules, would entail much higher costs. However, this negative dynamic for the crowd is balanced by the already mentioned opportunity to perform a more rewarding work compared to ordinary activities and to assert its importance at different stages of the value production chain, which also guarantees the client company to reduce the risk of a lack of motivation to participate in the crowdsourcing project.

Finally, a significant criticism of this model concerns the rights of intellectual property, in the absence of an employment contract between the members of the crowd involved in the crowdsourcing activities and the client company. It is important to underline, on the one hand, the lawfulness for the company to benefit from the spontaneous contributions received from the crowd, and on the other hand, the unacceptability from the ethical point of view of an exploitation of the same in generating profit, without paying those who produced them. Before the start of the process, it is therefore essential to establish the mechanisms of governance of intellectual property, legal, and payment aspects [32]. A further risk—mentioned above—partly linked to this problem and, more specifically, to incentive techniques, is the contribution of low quality work or even the possible lack of participation; the latter is therefore a crucial challenge in defining how to manage crowdsourcing.

4. Managerial implications and conclusions

Flexibility and adaptability are essential elements for a fashion company to survive in this industry, which is characterized by market changes most significant and rapid compared to the past. Historically, fashion companies based their businesses on the designer's own creativity and experience. In fact, traditionally, design is a valuable strategic asset that is directly related to the competitive advantage of each player acting in this industry. This leads to emphasize the tacit knowledge derived from the experiences, perceptions, and expectations of an individual actor, namely the creative director.

Nonetheless, customers nowadays are looking for more differentiated and personalized products and they less and less recognize themselves in the traditional collections provided seasonally by fashion companies.

Based on this consideration, the fashion industry is seeking alternative and sustainable ways for growth. Among the existing alternatives, open innovation seems to be one of the most fruitful opportunities. The term open innovation refers to the use of external knowledge to emphasize internal creativity with the final aim to expand the market reach [11, 33]. In fact, by openly embracing open innovation, firms can leverage beyond their own resources and develop better ideas faster and at a lower cost. Along this conceptual framework, crowdsourcing is an effective means to implement open innovation strategies.

The use of crowdsourcing provides firms with several advantages. First, a company can save cost and time, since crowdsourcing does not require additional internal resources neither to plan nor realize outsourcing strategies. Moreover, thanks to the participation of a larger number of actors, the time to market can register significant reduction. Second, through crowdsourcing, firms can avoid any risk connected to the path dependency problem, opening the ideation process to a wider range of stimuli and opportunities. Third, thanks to the active consumer participation, firms can increase their loyalty to the brand and their attachment to the product. Finally, firms can profit of the possibility to better understand tastes and preferences of their customer and monitor the trend over the time.

Thanks to the implementation of crowdsourcing activities, various business models are popping up from the public's ideas, modifying the traditional structure of the fashion industry at every level of the value chain. The common element among these numerous and diverse business model configurations is the active role of external stakeholder, especially referring to customers. Engaging the current and potential customers is a good instrument to cope with the growing competition that characterized the fashion industry. This is especially true at an earlier stage of the firms' life cycle; in fact, a strong customer engagement can represent a competitive driver for a new venture. In other words, crowdsourcing provides start-ups with a new way to run their business, lowering the barriers for entry and introducing new critical success factors. Nevertheless, also incumbents can benefit from the involvement of customers in their decision processes with the final aim to draw them closer to their brands. Indeed, ideally in the brand's mind, consumers will be more loyal once they have contributed to build a product.

Author details

Luigi Nasta* and Luca Pirolo
LUISS – Libera Università Internazionale degli Studi Sociali Guido Carli, Rome, Italy

*Address all correspondence to: lnasta@luiss.it

References

[1] Howe J. Crowdsourcing. Il valore partecipativo come risorsa per il futuro del business. Bologna: Luca Sossella Editore; 2010

[2] Pellegrini B. Il crowdsourcing e il valore partecipativo. In: Howe J, editor. Crowdsourcing. Il valore partecipativo come risorsa per il futuro del business. Bologna: Luca Sossella Editore; 2010

[3] Pirolo L, Giustiniano L, Nenni ME. The Italian footwear industry: An empirical analysis. International Journal of Engineering Business Management. 2013;**5**:34

[4] Kotler P. The Prosumer Movement: A New Challenge For Marketers. In: Lutz RJ, editor. NA - Advances in Consumer Research. Provo, UT: Association for Consumer Research; 1986;**13**:510-513

[5] Von Hippel E. The Sources of Innovation. Oxford: Oxford University Press; 1988

[6] Piller FT, Moeslein K, Stotko CM. Does mass customization pay? An economic approach to evaluate customer integration. Production Planning and Control. 2004;**15**(4):435-444

[7] Zipkin P. Mass customization. MIT Sloan Management Review; 2001

[8] Von Hippel E. Democratizing Innovation. Cambridge (Massachusetts, USA): MIT Press; 2005

[9] Seltzer E, Mahmoudi D. Citizen participation, open innovation and crowdsourcing: Challenges and opportunities for planning. Journal of Planning Literature. 2012;**28**(1):3-18

[10] Leadbeater C, Miller P. The Pro-Am Revolution: How Enthusiasts Are Changing our Society and Economy. London: Demos; 2004. p. 24

[11] Chesbrough H. Open Innovation. Boston: Harvard Business Press; 2003

[12] Marchegiani L, Pirolo L. The proximity paradox: How localization influences relational exchange and innovation diffusion. Evidences from a cluster level analysis. An Enterprise Odyssey. International Conference Proceedings; 2004

[13] Pirolo L, Presutti M. Towards a dynamic knowledge-based approach to the innovation process: An empirical investigation on social capital inside an industrial cluster. International Journal of Learning and Intellectual Capital. 2007;**4**(1-2):147-173

[14] Felin T, Zenger TR. Closed or open innovation? Problem solving and the governance choice. Research Policy. 2014;**43**(5):914-925

[15] Chesbrough H. Managing Open Innovation. Research-Technology Management. 2004;**47**(1):23-26

[16] Gassmann O, Enkel E. Towards a theory of open innovation: Three core process archetypes. Proceedings of the RADMA Conference; 2004

[17] Speidel KP. Problem description in open problem solving: How to overcome cognitive and psychological roadblocks. In: Sloane P, editor. A Guide to Open Innovation and Crowdsourcing. Advice from Leading Experts. London: Koganpage; 2011

[18] Zhao Y, Zhu Q. Evaluation on crowdsourcing research: Current status and future direction. Information Systems Frontiers. 2012;**16**(3):417-434

[19] Brabham DC. Crowdsourcing as a model for problem solving. Convergence: The International Journal of Research into New Media Technologies. 2008;**14**(1):75-90

[20] Christopher M, Lowson R, Peck H. Creating agile supply chains in the fashion industry. International Journal of Retail & Distribution Management. 2004;**32**(8):367-376

[21] Ostrom E. In: Page Scott E, editor. The Difference: How the Power of Diversity Creates Better Groups, Firms, Schools, and Societies. Princeton: Princeton University Press; 2008, 2007. 448p. Perspectives on Politics, 6(4), 828-829

[22] Page SE. The Difference. How the Power of Diversity Creates Better Groups, Firms, Schools and Societies. Princeton (New Jersey, USA): Princeton University Press; 2007

[23] Nasta L, Pirolo L, Wikström P. Diversity in creative teams: A theoretical framework and a research methodology for the analysis of the music industry. Creative Industries Journal. 2016;**9**(2):97-106

[24] Lakhani, Karim, Jeppesen, Lohse, Panetta. The Value of Openness in Scientific Problem Solving. Working Paper 07-050. Harvard Business School; 2007

[25] Nenni ME, Giustiniano L, Pirolo L. Demand forecasting in the fashion industry: A review. International Journal of Engineering Business Management. 2013;**5**(Godište 2013):5-36

[26] D'amico S, Giustiniano L, Nenni ME, Pirolo L. Product lifecycle management and compliance with international standards: A case study analysis in the footwear industry. International Journal of Product Lifecycle Management. 2014;**7**(2-3):215-229

[27] Corbo L, Pirolo L, Rodrigues V. Business model adaptation in response to an exogenous shock: An empirical analysis of the Portuguese footwear industry. International Journal of Engineering Business Management. 2018;**10**:1847979018772742

[28] Estrelle-Arolas E, González-Ladrón-De-Guevara F. Towards an integrated crowdsourcing definition. Journal of Information Science. 2012;**38**(2):189-200

[29] Pedersen J, Kocsis D, Tripathi A, Tarrell A, Weerakoon A, Tahmasbi N, et al., Conceptual foundations of crowdsourcing: A review of IS research. 46th Hawaii International Conference on System Sciences; 2013

[30] Schenk E, Guittard C. Crowdsourcing: What can be outsourced to the crowd, and why. In: Workshop on Open Source Innovation, Strasbourg, France. Vol. 72; 2009. p. 3

[31] Root-Bernstein RS. Discovering, Inventing and Solving Problems at the Frontiers of Knowledge. Cambridge: Harvard Business Press; 1989

[32] Vukovic M. Crowdsourcing for enterprises. In: Services-I, 2009 World Conference on. IEEE; 2009. pp. 686-692

[33] Chesbrough HW, Teece DJ. Organizing for innovation: when is virtual virtuous? In: The Transfer and Licensing of Know-How and Intellectual Property: Understanding the Multinational Enterprise in the Modern World; 2008. pp. 335-341

Chapter 4

From Individual Creativity to Team-Based Creativity

Margarida Romero

Abstract

Supporting the development of creative competency is important for the actual challenges of the society. However, creativity has been mainly approached in an individual way, without considering the specificities of team-based creativity processes. In this chapter, we establish the differences between creativity as an individual approach and creativity as a collaborative process. Then we discuss creativity from the perspective of the leaners' and teachers' attitudes. Subsequently, we discuss the concept of the *margin of creativity* in different learning activities. We finalize this chapter by discussing digital uses that can support creativity in team-based contexts.

Keywords: creativity, co-creativity, team-based creativity, social creativity, problem-solving

1. Introduction

Creativity is a key competency in addressing the social challenges of postindustrial knowledge societies [1] in which new jobs have an increasing need to be supported by the creative class [2], in which individuals who work in it "engage in complex problem-solving that involves a great deal of independent judgment and requires high levels of education or human capital" (p. 8). In a context of a growing influence of automatization and artificial intelligence, creativity is being widely recognized as an important competency which makes a difference between humans and robotic work [2–4]. For Florida [2], creativity is a factor of socioeconomic differentiation of contemporary societies between "creative classes," who develop occupations where creativity is a determining factor in their complex problem-solving activities, and other social classes in which routine work could be easier to replace through automatization technologies. The noncreative class is in risk to face a growing precariousness within urban environments in which the creative class took the urban space. The importance of creativity as a new imperative of competitiveness is emphasized by Peck [5] as a manifestation of neoliberalism that would tend to increase competition within the active class and demands a higher level of creative problem-solving competency to increase the productivity and innovation to face the optimization of the industrial and service-oriented activities being challenged by automatization and globalization. However, despite the pression for developing creativity to face the twenty-first century challenges [6] and despite the growing differences between "creative classes" and others citizens [2], creativity is still not an educational priority in most of the educational systems of the OECD [7, 8].

2. Creativity is demanding

Creativity is often perceived negatively in educational settings [9]. Teachers and learners sometimes associate creativity with creative processes that have no purpose and no constraints that can lead to worthless solutions. They associate creativity to tasks in which the *margin of creativity* offers an extensive number of solutions, without considering the creative process in some activities with a limited, but important, margin of creativity in the domains such language, physics, or mathematics. Despite the misconception associating creativity to effortless artistic processes [8], creativity is a demanding process resulting from a good analysis of the situation-problem and its context, which must then lead to a solution. Creativity is about creating an innovative, relevant, and valuable solution [10] that is parsimonious and elegant in the face of an initial situation-problem.

3. From creativity as an individual trait to collaborative creativity

Creativity is often seen as an individual trait that can be manifested both in the process and the product or artifact created through the creative process [4]. While everyone has a different level of development of the creativity competency, all subjects can develop their creative potential [10] by developing a better awareness of the creative processes such as divergent thinking [11] and also the creative criteria to self-regulate the quality of the creative solution. Creativity has been mostly studied from an individual point of view in the field of psychology, but there are a growing number of studies in the field of education, not only in individual tasks but also in team-based activities engaging students in different types of creative projects. When learners face complex problems that require collaboration and creativity, then creativity is a social process. If we talk about distributed cognition, we can also talk about distributed creativity [12]. In the educational context, creativity has been mainly analyzed with the help of individual activities [13], which goes against the social character of creativity [14] but also opportunities for collaboration in the context of learning involving tasks of a certain complexity [15]. We see creativity as an iterative process that can develop both individually and collaboratively [16]. Constraints are sometimes a trigger for the initial creative process; creating with limited resources establishes a framework that leads the learner to engage in a creative process to successfully meet these requirements; during the creative process, the learner must explore several new solutions to a problem, to draw inspiration from other realizations to guide one's reasoning and finally to select a solution while considering the context of the situation-problem. This definition of the creative process fostered by a situational problem coincides with Vygotsky's concept of double simulation, according to which learners overcome critical conflicts by making use of cultural artifacts in order to create a solution that emancipates them from the problem situation [17].

4. *Creatitude* as a willingness to engage in creative solutions

This creative attitude or *creatitude* goes beyond the acquisition and understanding of knowledge to give an active role to the learner. Our creativity invites us to invest in creative activities in which we (co) construct cultural products of different types. *Creatitude* refers to the willingness to try new approaches and solutions and also to the ability to make critical and benevolent judgments about the process and to make new attempts when creative attempts are not of enough quality. From the written creation to robot programming, creative attitude is a way to interact in the world and overcome the consumer or passive role of humans not nurturing their creative attitude toward the problem situations they experience in their lives. Creative attitude allows us to develop new approaches and develop various solutions to problems that challenge us in a way that was not initially expected.

Creating is not enough; creative process should propose an efficient solution that is deemed valid by a reference group. Creativity is socioculturally rooted and cannot be only designated by the subject having to create something but by the community or reference group who will evaluate the value and relevance of the solution in a certain context.

Creative solutions should be not only original but also valuable. In instance, making a chocolate salad is perhaps original, but if it does not taste good, it is not a good creative solution. Creativity is part of a design process and involves a reasonable use of resources. It might be thought that equipping automobiles with six wheels is an original invention and that the two extra wheels add stability to the vehicle, but if these new cars use more resources than necessary, they are not a good creative solution. So, there is a difference between originality and creativity. If originality is a potential for creativity, it is not its only component. This originality must therefore be oriented toward an iterative and complex, rational process of reflection that requires the efforts of learners.

Creativity also requires the learner to engage in decision -making about the way he analyzes the situation and decisions on the process to follow to develop a solution. Creativity emerges in a context in which the learner must decide the way he will proceed individually or negotiate the way they will proceed as a team in co-creative learning activities. In creative process we cannot always apply established solutions for which we can follow recipes step by step or copy a certain procedure. This is what we do most often in class. To pick up the example in the culinary world, being a good cook is not about running existing recipes but about being able to match flavors in innovative ways. In this sense, creative attitude or *creatitude* refers to the willingness to try new approaches and solutions and also the ability to make critical and benevolent judgments about the process and to make new attempts when creative attempts are not of enough quality. It is important not to think that *creatitude* is only an innate quality that only eccentric people can possess. How many times have we heard "I'm not creative. I am Cartesian." Being creative is an attitude and a competency that develops by engaging in motivating projects in which we have real power of action and influence over the world around us.

5. The margin of creativity as an educational design tool

Despite the increasing awareness on the need to develop learners' creativity for today's society, it is difficult for teachers to put creativity as a priority in the context of standardized tests that rules the main milestones of the school curriculum. Therefore, we consider the development of creativity as a *margin* when teachers conceptualize their pedagogical sequences. By *margin of creativity*, we refer to the number of creative possibilities offered by elements such as the domain-specific knowledge of the task, the context of the class, and the time offered for the development of creativity among many other factors having the possibility to affect the activity. It is up to the teacher to judge the moment, the subject, and the context to determine how the development of creativity can be effectively integrated into the activities. In addition, it is important to distinguish the margin of creativity in the solution to be created and the margin of creativity in the creation process. Sometimes the pedagogical context offers more flexibility in the production to be done and sometimes more flexibility in the process of realization. For example, when programming for the first time with software like Scratch, learners can make different productions, but they will have to work with the same blocks of code. Learners can create a story, a game, or a quiz. Conversely, the teacher may decide that learners should all create a story but leave them the choice of the best medium to tell their story supporting learners' agency. Learners can thus do theater with robots, create a book with augmented reality, create an audiovisual journey with virtual reality, or glue electrical components on puppets.

Moreover, although creativity is a crucial competency to develop in learners, it does not mean that learners must always be creative. The balance between conventional thinking and creative thinking is a more realistic goal. Some educational objectives can be better achieved by conventional ways of thinking. When learners want to understand specific French rules such as color adjectives, the teacher must conform to French conventions (even if it is possible to find a creative way to teach them these rules!). Teachers must also follow a prescribed curriculum, even if it can be applied flexibly. It is by considering these aspects that the psychologist of education at the University of Georgia, Mark Runco says that teachers should aim to develop post-conventional thinking [11]. This thinking refers to the ability of learners to understand established conventions while being able to make creative decisions emerging from a personal reflection process. Post-conventional thinking also refers to the learners' ability to understand context that is more supportive to creativity and contexts that are more conducive to conventional thinking. By focusing on the development of creativity while enabling learners to understand the contexts conducive to creativity, we will be able to get learners to understand that creativity is a competency that can develop in everyone and that must be deployed in the context in which we evolve. Context awareness and empathy are important aspects of creativity as a contextual process [18].

6. Creativity in all disciplines

Creativity is more naturally associated to the artistic domains such the visual arts or literature. Despite this misconception, creativity can be developed in disciplines or domains that are not generally associated with creativity such as history, especially through the historical thinking approach [19] or science, through the maker education and STEAM approaches [18]. By considering the concept of creative margin, creativity can be developed through the study of discipline that may seem too rigid or based on immutable laws to let learners be creative and potentially miss important contents. History, for example, may seem too rigid when viewed as a mirror of the past. When viewed as an interpretative discipline where sources and testimonies serve as a breeding ground for fact-finding and development of deep understanding, then the historical inquiry process and the creative process have several points in common.

7. Creative uses of technology-enhanced learning (TEL)

We must distinguish digital uses that support the creativity of learners of digital uses that place the learner in a situation of passive consumption (like viewing educational videos) or interactive consumption (like quizzes). Based on the model of cognitive engagement developed by Chi and Wylie [20], we have developed a model of creative engagement through the use of technology-enhanced learning (TEL): the passive-participatory model [21] (**Figure 1**).

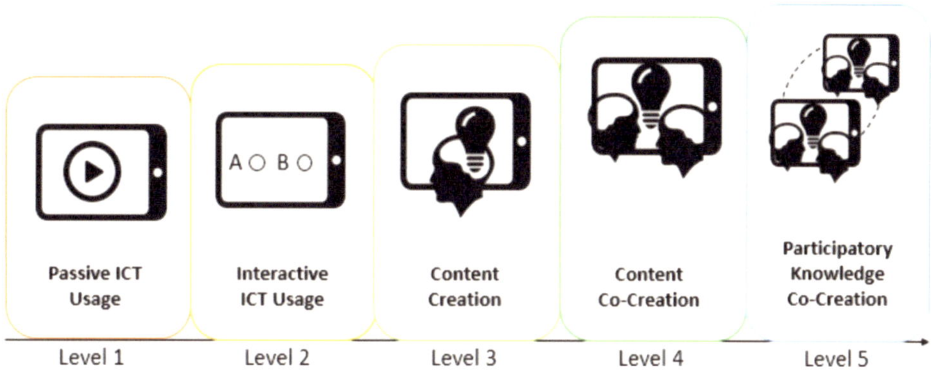

Figure 1.
Levels of creative engagement in the passive-participatory model [21].

In the passive-participatory model [21], we distinguish five types of uses of technology-enhanced learning according to the creative engagement of the learner: passive ICT usage, interactive ICT usage, individual content creation, co-creation of content, and, ultimately, participatory knowledge-based co-creation geared toward understanding or solving problems shared within a learning community. When learners are engaged in co-creative activities (levels 4 and 5), they share their experiences and knowledge, then they negotiate their relevance within the group over the problem they seek to understand and solve. In co-creative activities, learners are required to discuss more explicitly their ideas, decisions and evaluation of the intermediate solutions. By going through a more explicit process, learners can benefit from the creative think-aloud process of their team-mates. This process can lead participants to produce new content based on explanations provided or exposure to peer knowledge designs [22]. Such original productions then become digital media artifacts, such as text-based creations (e.g., when posted to a wiki), audiovisual creations (e.g., interactive video), multimedia (e.g., digital storytelling), or a computer program (e.g., Scratch visual programming).

8. Activities supporting the creative uses of technologies

The uses of digital technologies do not automatically generate an increase in the quality of the learning activities or the performances; neither can we assume the positive effect of technologies in the creative processes and outcomes. The scientific literature offers several principles to consider when it comes to co-creation with digital technologies. The benefits of teamwork must first exceed the transaction costs of coordination and communication actions [23]. In addition, when using technologies collaboratively, it is important that the physical or digital environment [24] is conducive to interaction and that the teacher offers scaffolding to learners while modeling the competencies and attitudes required to correctly collaborate. Teachers should encourage leadership to promote the production and negotiation of meaning in learners [25]. Collaboration among learners should also allow for a mutual and sustained understanding of the object of study [26–28] where there are no restful interactions on a dynamic of domination or idea accumulation without arguments between the members of the team [29]. Moreover, Wegerif [30] emphasizes that it is important to consider the ways in which learners can interact online when the development of competencies is the main pedagogical intent, as is the case in this research. Thus, when collaborating with digital tools, the learner must have a space to step back and actively listen to other members' opinions, with the aim of creating a dialogue space for reflection [30]. The dialogical space in collaborative tools should be able to support the team-mates' discussion about their different perspectives, opinions, and ideas [31]. Supporting the team-mates' discussion can contribute to their understanding of intersubjectivity [32] during the co-creative process. The mediating tools [33] and the community also participate in structuring collaborative inquiry processes [34] to understand the shared object. As for the composition of the group, Webb and Palincsar [35] argue that heterogeneous groups in terms of expertise can be more productive in collaborative tasks. For effective collaboration, team members must also share responsibility for the learning process and shared purpose [36]. It is also important to pay attention to over-structuring the pedagogical sequence that can create a scripted collaboration [37] that does not have as much pedagogical potential. When properly designed and implemented, the collaborative use of educational technologies would allow learners to experience more achievements, to master more fact-based information, and to be better able to solve problems than when learning for individual use [38–40]. Learners also show a more positive attitude toward the subject and are more motivated to learn when they collaborate with the technologies than when they use them individually [40, 41]. Collaborative idea creation thus enables the advancement and enrichment of the ideas of the learner community and also allows the development of deep understanding [42]. The idea of creating knowledge is thus very important in the design of the collaboration.

9. Conclusion

Developing creative competency for learners and teachers at the same time is an important goal of the educational system and lifelong learning to prepare younger generations to be the creators of knowledge, analysts, leaders, designers, digital citizens, computational thinkers, and the people of tomorrow. It is essential that this aim be reflected in the design of pedagogical sequences built by teachers and lived by learners to train children to the increased complexity of our world. Developing creativity competency is achieved through complex, creative, contextualized, dynamic, digital uses that transform the way we teach and, above all, transform the way learners learn [43]. Within this chapter, we have stressed the importance of moving from an individual way of developing creativity competency to embrace a more collective approach of this competency in order to increase the society capacity to better solve team-level challenges and also increase the citizens' capabilities to deal with societal and global challenges requiring the subject to engage in a creative attitude to overcome current difficulties.

Acknowledgements

This study was supported by the CreaMaker project funded by the Agence Nationale de la Recherche (ANR) in France (ANR-18-CE38-0001).

Conflict of interest

The author declares no conflict of interest.

DOI: http://dx.doi.org/10.5772/intechopen.89126

Author details

Margarida Romero
Laboratoire d'Innovation et Numérique pour l'Education, Université Côte d'Azur, Nice, France

*Address all correspondence to: margarida.romero@univ-cotedazur.fr

References

[1] Garrison DR. E-learning in the 21st Century: A Framework for Research and Practice. [Internet]. 2nd ed. New York, NY, USA: Routledge; 2011 [cited 2019 Aug 30]. Available from: https://www.taylorfrancis.com/books/9780203838761

[2] Florida RL. The rise of the creative class: and how it's transforming work, leisure, community and everyday life. Nachdr. New York, NY: Basic Books; 2006. p. 434

[3] De Bono E. Serious creativity: using the power of lateral thinking to create new ideas. New York, NY, USA: Penguin Random House; 2015

[4] Sternberg RJ, Lubart TI. Defying the Crowd: Cultivating Creativity in a Culture of Conformity. Free Press; 1995

[5] Peck J. Struggling with the creative class. International Journal of Urban and Regional Research. 2005;**29**(4):740-770

[6] Hesse F, Care E, Buder J, Sassenberg K, Griffin P. A framework for teachable collaborative problem solving skills. In: Griffin P, Care E, editors. Assessment and Teaching of 21st Century Skills [Internet]. Dordrecht, Netherlands: Springer; 2015. [cited 2019 Aug 30]. p. 37-56. Available from: http://link.springer.com/10.1007/978-94-017-9395-7_2

[7] Durpaire F, Mabilon-Bonfils B. La fin de l'école: l'ère du savoir-relation. 1re édition. Paris: Presses universitaires de France; 2014. 273 p

[8] Capron Puozzo I. La créativité en éducation et formation: Perspectives théoriques et pratiques. De Boeck. Louvain-la-Neuve, Belgium; 2017

[9] Lytton H. Creativity and Education. [Internet]. London: Routledge; 2012. [cited 2019 Aug 30]. Available from: https://ezproxy.aub.edu.lb/login?url=https://www.taylorfrancis.com/books/9781136669699

[10] Runco MA. Creativity and education. New Horizons in Education. 2008;**56**(1):n1

[11] Runco MA. Divergent thinking and creative potential. Perspectives on Creativity Research. New York, NY: Hampton Press; 2013. 425 p

[12] Sawyer RK, DeZutter S. Distributed creativity: How collective creations emerge from collaboration. Psychology of Aesthetics, Creativity, and the Arts. 2009;**3**(2):81

[13] Romero M, Hyvönen P, Barberà E. Creativity in collaborative learning across the life span. Creative Education. 2012;**3**(4):422-429

[14] Fischer G, Giaccardi E, Eden H, Sugimoto M, Ye Y. Beyond binary choices: Integrating individual and social creativity. International Journal of Human Computer Studies. 2005;**63**(4):482-512

[15] Kirschner F, Paas F, Kirschner PA. A cognitive load approach to collaborative learning: United brains for complex tasks. Educational Psychology Review. 2009;**21**(1):31-42

[16] Mouchiroud C, Lubart T. Social creativity: A cross-sectional study of 6-to 11-year-old children. International Journal of Behavioral Development. 2002;**26**(1):60-69

[17] Vygotsky LS, Rieber R, Carton A. The Collected Works of LS Vygotsky: The History of the Development of Higher Mental Functions. Vol. 4. New York: Plenum Press; 1997

[18] Barma S, Romero M, Deslandes R. Implementing maker spaces to promote cross-generational sharing and learning. In: Romero M, Sawchuk K, Blat J, Sayago S, Ouellet H, editors. Game-based learning across the lifespan:

cross-generational and age-oriented topics. Cham: Springer; 2017. p. 65-78

[19] Lille B, Romero M. Creativity assessment in the context of maker-based projects. Design and Technology Education: An International Journal. 2017;**22**(3):32-47

[20] Chi MTH, Wylie R. The ICAP framework: Linking cognitive engagement to active learning outcomes. Educational Psychologist. 2014;**49**(4):219-243

[21] Romero M, Laferriere T, Power TM. The move is on! From the passive multimedia learner to the engaged co-creator. eLearn. 2016;**2016**(3):1

[22] Nizet I, Laferrière T. Description des modes spontanés de co-construction de connaissances: contributions à un forum électronique axé sur la pratique réflexive. Recherche & Formation. 2005;**48**:151-166

[23] Kirschner P, Kirschner F, Janssen J. The collaboration principle in multimedia learning. The Cambridge Handbook of Multimedia Learning. 2014:547-575

[24] O'Donnell AM. Structuring dyadic interaction through scripted cooperation. Cognitive Perspectives on Peer Learning. 1999:179-196

[25] Pea RD. The social and technological dimensions of scaffolding and related theoretical concepts for learning, education, and human activity. The Journal of the Learning Sciences. 2004;**13**(3):423-451

[26] Arrighi C, Ferrario R. Abductive reasoning, interpretation and collaborative processes. Foundations of Science. 2008;**13**(1):75-87

[27] Clark HH, Wilkes-Gibbs D. Referring as a collaborative process. Cognition. 1986;**22**(1):1-39

[28] Roschelle J. Learning by collaborating: Convergent conceptual change. The Journal of the Learning Sciences. 1992;**2**(3):235-276

[29] Mercer N. The guided construction of knowledge: talk amongst teachers and learners. Clevedon, Avon, England ; Philadelphia: Multilingual Matters; 1995. 135 p

[30] Wegerif R. A dialogic understanding of the relationship between CSCL and teaching thinking skills. International Journal of Computer-Supported Collaborative Learning. 2006;**1**(1):143-157

[31] Dillenbourg P, Baker MJ, Blaye A, O'Malley C. The Evolution of Research on Collaborative Learning. Oxford: Elsevier; 1995

[32] Koschmann T. Dewey's contribution to the foundations of CSCL research. In: Proceedings of the Conference on Computer Support for Collaborative Learning: Foundations for a CSCL Community; International Society of the Learning Sciences; 2002. pp. 17-22

[33] Vygotsky LS. Mind and Society: The Development of Higher Mental Processes. Cambridge, MA: Harvard University Press; 1978

[34] Sami P, Kai H. From meaning making to joint construction of knowledge practices and artefacts: A trialogical approach to CSCL. In: Proceedings of the 9th International Conference on Computer Supported Collaborative Learning-Volume 1; International Society of the Learning Sciences; 2009. pp. 83-92

[35] Webb NM, Palincsar AS. Group Processes in the Classroom. In: Handbook of educational psychology. London, England: Prentice Hall International; 1996. p. 841-873

[36] Fransen J, Weinberger A, Kirschner PA. Team effectiveness and

team development in CSCL. Educational Psychologist. 2013;**48**(1):9-24

[37] Dillenbourg P. Over-Scripting CSCL: The Risks of Blending Collaborative Learning with Instructional Design. Heerlen: Open Universiteit Nederland; 2002

[38] Johnson DW, Johnson RT. Cooperation and Competition: Theory and Research. MN, US: Interaction Book Company; 1989;viii:253

[39] Johnson DW, Johnson RT, Smith KA. Cooperative learning returns to college what evidence is there that it works? Change: The Magazine of Higher Learning. 1998;**30**(4):26-35

[40] Resta P, Laferrière T. Technology in support of collaborative learning. Educational Psychology Review. 2007;**19**(1):65-83

[41] Springer L, Stanne ME, Donovan SS. Effects of small-group learning on undergraduates in science, mathematics, engineering, and technology: A meta-analysis. Review of Educational Research. 1999;**69**(1):21-51

[42] Wiske MS, Sick M, Wirsig S. New technologies to support teaching for understanding. International Journal of Educational Research. 2001;**35**(5):483-501

[43] Kamga R, Romero M, Komis V, Mirsili A. Design requirements for educational robotics activities for sustaining collaborative problem solving. In: International Conference EduRobotics 2016; Springer, Cham; 2016. pp. 225-228

Section 2

Creativity in Machines

Chapter 5

Shared Futures: An Exploration of the Collaborative Potential of Intelligent Machines and Human Ingenuity in Cocreating Value

Teboho Pitso

Abstract

This chapter reports on the exploratory study that aimed at better understanding the conditions under which the combined capabilities of intelligent technologies and human ingenuity could be harnessed to create new efficiencies. The study was conducted within a university setting as universities should model how future societies ought to look like and drive societal change. As the new digital society 5.0 takes shape, the time has come to critically probe one aspect of society 5.0, the leveraging of human-machine collaborations to generate unique ideas and convert them into tangible results. The sequential mixed methods' approach together with a sociocultural lens was used to investigate the ideal university conditions that could foster human-machine collaborations in value cocreation. Nineteen Senior Scandinavian and South African managers were interviewed to elicit their views on how human-machine collaborations could be harnessed to cocreate value within complex university settings. Entrenched cultures, policies, systems, and multiple stakeholder interests which complex into rules and routines mostly define university mores. These university mores are often impervious to rapid newness and radical change. Fifteen advanced undergraduates at one South African university also participated in a quasi-experimentation that investigated team formation and team development within the context of human-machine collaborations.

Keywords: value cocreation, intelligent machines, human ingenuity, human-machine collaboration, sociocultural perspective

1. Introduction

Intelligent technologies represent a major shift in the capabilities of computing machines from performing repetitive tasks within the mainly quiescent algorithmic problem-solving frameworks towards generating smarter solutions through the use of advanced heuristics and active interaction with humans. Algorithmic frameworks are considered quiescent when they rely on a specific set of instructions that totally reproduce expected outputs. The capabilities of intelligent technologies that are most likely to contribute in creative problem-solving, deep learning required in creativity and new discoveries with potential to create value require huge data processing, multiple iteration abilities and huge resource commitment. These three conditionalities of creative machines would enable these machines to generate advanced heuristics that can produce smarter solutions that might still lack formal proofs of their veracity and efficiency in practical situations. The testing of the correctness of the machine-generated solutions and their efficacy in resolving real, practical problems falls within the human realm. This is one area of collaboration between machines and humans. Other areas of collaboration between machines and humans relate to the inability of machines to adapt to real environmental changes, inability to frame and define complex problems as well as inability of machines to negotiate the complex sociocultural realities that can facilitate the adoption of machine-generated solutions in specific organisational contexts. The latter area of human-machine collaborations was the focus of the study that is reported in this chapter. The study sought to understand better the organisational conditions that could enable the adoption of machine-generated solutions and, by extension, those organisational conditions that could be inimical to the use of such solutions. Through the use of a sociocultural lens, the possibilities of human-machine collaborations are first explored through eliciting the perspectives and experiences of senior university managers in areas of innovation and entrepreneurship. Creativity was assumed, in the study, as the plinth of innovation and entrepreneurship; hence, focus was on the realities of key senior players in innovation and entrepreneurship as they actuate in real university spaces. Universities are considered as complex spaces where entrenched cultures that subsume taken-for-granted social mores, systems and policies as well as multiple stakeholder interests determine the activities and strategic directions of the university. Universities across the globe have already adopted technological solutions in varying degrees of sophistication, and some scholars have critiqued the fetishist and ideological manner of their adoption in universities [1]. Some of the major concerns include:

- That university technological response tends to be framed in ways that endow technology with magical power that is capable of resolving protracted problems of academic practices. This framing remains undertheorised and mostly empirically undertested such that it assumes an ideological posture and a marketing-like puffery which attracts scholarly and intellectual critique.

- That technology tends to influence university policies and systems in ways that upset deeply entrenched academic cultures of autonomy and professional identities such that academic autonomy and professional identities get reduced to bureaucratic and technocratic logic [2]. Understood this way, academic autonomy and professional identities are positioned as subordinate to technology without substantial logical and empirical justifications. This subordinated positioning of academic shrines (autonomy and identity) mostly considered as sacrosanct in academia would most likely affect the smooth transition of universities to the cyber-physical spaces of society 5.0. Society 5.0 relies on greater convergence between virtual and real spaces such that a proper understanding of the sociocultural nature of the real spaces is essential in human progression towards society 5.0 which leverages closer collaborations between these cyber-physical spaces. While information society 4.0 relied on the cloud technologies facilitated through the internet to store, retrieve and analyse data, society 5.0 will depend on intelligent technologies to process and interpret big swathes of data elicited through sensors in the physical space which would then be used to suggest and help in cocreation of new value propositions. Knowledge and theorisation around the virtual and real spaces in terms of creating ideal conditions for greater synergy and collaborations between these spaces would be essential in the realisation of society 5.0. The study that is being reported in this chapter makes a modest contribution towards understanding the complexities involved in making society 5.0 possible.

Added to these ideologising concerns around technology is the general marginalisation of creativity, innovation and entrepreneurship in the core academic practices. The entrenched academic cultures tend to sideline human creativity, and the human-machine creativity would find it even harder to negotiate a space within the entrenched strategic core of university curricula. In this sense, there are strong indications that without appreciating the sociocultural aspect of enacting human-machine creativity in universities and even other organisations, human-machine creativity would remain on the margins of such institutions or organisations. It is, in this sense, that the collaborative potential of intelligent machines and human ingenuity as mapping out within a university context was examined through perspectives of key role players in university innovation and entrepreneurship units. This collaborative potential was also examined in terms of the extent to which it impacted team formation and development. The variant of Tuckman's Stages of Team Development [3] as expounded by Crosta and McConnell [4] was used as the basis of analysis. The study is thus a subfield that falls somewhere between the emerging scholarship of artificial intelligence and human psychology within the socio-cognitivist traditions that recognise the value of teamwork in creativity. In the next section, an understanding of the historical trajectory of artificial intelligence and its recent forages into the hallowed spaces of human creativity is developed. Furthermore, understandings of the limits of creative machines which open up possibilities of human-machine collaborations are explored in ways that locate the study in these debates. These debates are then further processed within two main psychological concepts of sociocultural perspective and stages of team development.

2. Framing the study

2.1 Society 5.0

Noted as the supersmart service society and still essentially human-centred, society 5.0 combines innovation, education and social action to generate new value using human-machine capabilities [4–6]. It leverages unprecedented progress in technological advances that allow for human-machine interaction and possible collaboration to cocreate new value propositions that disrupt the current societal and business practices plinth (**Figure 1**).

In a powerful book called *Futureproof*, Minter and Storkey [7] identify 15 forces that will shape society 5.0 and disrupt current societal practices. Three of these forces relate to the mindset and the rest on technological advances. This emphasis on the mindset and technological savvy in shaping society 5.0 illuminates stronger synergistic relations between human psychology and advanced information technologies (IT) that will define society 5.0. Society 5.0 will not be defined by the dominance of intelligent machines over humans but will see greater human-machine collaborations that deliver innovation that result in the creation of a supersmart service society and the galvanising of a quinary economic sector (**Figure 1**). A quinary economic sector is noted mainly for disrupting and reorganising economic activities of the primary, secondary, tertiary and quaternary sectors [2], leveraging big data analytics and relying upon new technologies to create superior human conveniences. There is thus a legitimate need to work on the

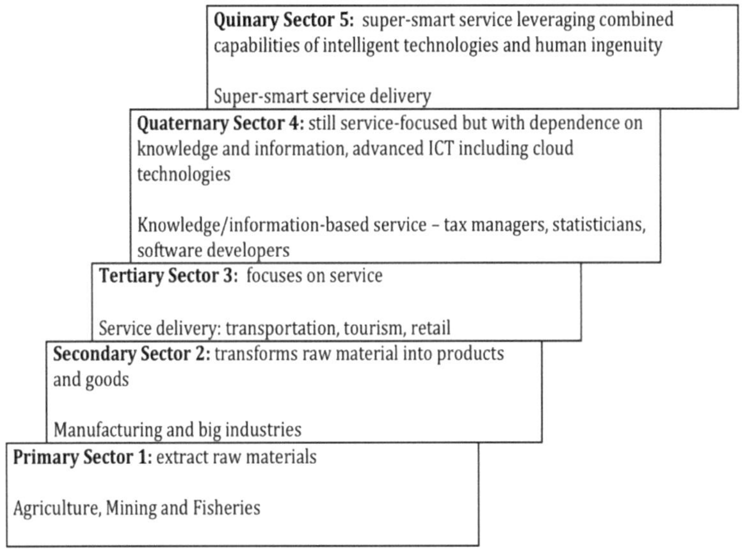

Figure 1.
The evolution of the economic sectors [2].

mindset of people in order to substantially increase their awareness level with regard to the changing nature of the relation between humans and technologies from quiescent to intellectual exchanges. These intellectual exchanges will enhance both the human and machine intelligences. This awareness begins with understanding human-machine interaction within the framework of artificial intelligences and then followed by exploring possibilities of human-machine collaboration that result in innovative ideas. A more growth-focused mindset will be needed if people are to cope and thrive in society 5.0. There is thus a need to develop an understanding of how such a mindset can be cultivated in order to prepare people for the future in which people interact and collaborate with smart machines. A terse historical background is essential so we could put the growth-focused mindset into perspective. Humans are 'puzzles of needs', and every society and its economic activities have been organised around meeting and, in most cases, even creating these needs so as to meet them most conveniently. Humans and tools have been at the heart of figuring out these puzzles of needs and meeting them in the most efficient way. We have termed different stages of solving these 'puzzles of needs' industrial epochs with each epoch building on the previous one and providing a better and more efficient way of dealing with these 'puzzles of needs' through the use of evolving technological advances. The first wave of these technological advances thought to have started in early twentieth century saw the dominance of standardised, routine industrial processes that were organised around assembly line and powered by human muscle as a proxy for real robots. Efficiency was achieved through the measurability of each step of the assembly line and fixed tasks that were sufficiently easy as to be performed by semi-skilled workers. These semi-skilled workers required little formal education and represented, in form and substance, some kind of 'Homo sapiens robots'. The second wave is set to have started in the early 1970s and reached its apotheosis in the 1990s. It is noted for its reliance on advanced information technologies with computers as its key cynosure, large databases and the onset of automation. This economic epoch is also noted for big machines that replaced human muscle as human muscle started increasingly losing its relevance in economic activity, but human cognitive abilities became increasingly sought-after in business and industry as the post-workerist era became a reality. University qualifications increasingly became the basis of securing employment with increased demand for 'fixed' graduate attributes that were purportedly sought-after by industry and business. While the third wave builds on the two waves, it offers an entirely new way of doing things. It leverages AI technologies and human ingenuity in such a way as to galvanise them into accessing real-time data to produce products and services that are highly individualised and optimised to meet human needs in the smartest way possible. It also extricates humans from tedious, standardised and routine work as robots can now assume that role which creates new roles for humans. The third wave thus sees the resurgence of human work albeit in new roles. These new human roles in industry and business will see greater collaboration between humans and smart machines as they collectively search, design, test and scale new or improved products and services, that is, engage actively in cocreation of value. These new work roles and human-machine collaborations will require an entirely new mindset and a new skills set. The 'fixed' mindset of the first and, to a certain extent, second wave will become redundant and obsolete in the next 5–25 years as new work roles emerge at an exponential pace. Dweck [8] argues that a growth-focused mindset thrives on challenges, persists in the face of formidable odds and embraces uncertainty as it innovates and adapts to changes on a continual basis. My strongest sense is that such a growth-focused mindset ought to constantly try out new things, experiment, fail, try again and be able to undertake research projects as it effectively works with highly discrete teams which also consist of non-humans. Society 5.0 will increasingly see the formation of such human-machine teams with AI technologies filtering and doing basic analysis of huge swathes of data and humans converting it into real value with benefits accruing to humans. This will require not only new sets of skills but new ways of thinking and doing things.

A good starting point would be on whether university leadership is ready for this mindset disruption and whether our students can cope with new projects that involve cocreating value with non-humans in the form of intelligent technologies. It was thus particularly important to tease out the readiness of university leadership to embrace the framework of society 5.0 in ways that compel:

- Reimagining university and curricular processes in ways that leverage AI technologies. This would require that universities move away from fixed mindsets that see very little value in creative problem-solving. There is an absolute need for universities to prepare students to collaborate with smart machines to generate new and better ideas that can be converted to tangible results. For the purpose of this chapter, this was a major focus, but there are many areas of university setup that are ready to be disrupted in order for universities to move into society 5.0. Societies rely on universities to prepare them for the next order of things, and it is thus incumbent upon universities to discharge this mandate without fail. Classroom routines can be automated and thus free human teachers from such tedious work and allow them to set up more research projects that involve discrete students-machine teams that engage in creative activities. Known knowledge opens itself up for automation with robots, smartphones and virtual learning providing lessons wherever students are with less concerns to attend classes in physical spaces. Human teachers could become industry, government and community consultants as they prepare society for society 5.0 which could become a serious cultural shock and pose new risks such as cybersecurity and ethics of human/robot behaviours that could be detrimental to humans.

- Establishing groundwork for human-machine collaborations that could help usher in the super smart service society.

- Rethinking the business of human-business relations in ways that ethically optimise redistribution of wealth, eliminate inequality and harmonise race relations.

Through interviews with university leadership in innovation hubs and entrepreneurship centres, I sought to better understand how universities in two different contexts reacted and prepared themselves for these mindset and operations disruptions. My sense was that how universities treated leadership in these university entities (hubs, centres) and how this leadership in university hubs and centres challenged entrenched university cultures would provide a preliminary framework of how university readied themselves for society 5.0 or, if you like, the age of AI. I also conducted the quasi-experimentation on how students related to smart machines that actively interact with them as equals. I used a simple AI technology version called Google Assistant mainly because it appeared to be a simple but more advanced interactive AI technology in comparison with a similar Apple assistant device called Siri. I opted for the simplest human-machine interaction because the purpose was more to determine the potential of human-machine collaboration especially the complexities of team development. This study was thus a baseline research on human-machine collaboration. It offers insights on how these possibilities of fusing human ingenuity with intelligent technologies could map out within a university setting. The study also sought to avoid presenting this chapter as a polemic for AI rather sought to provide a framework that could lead to theorisation around supercreativity as it pens out in a university setting. The realities of society 5.0 are already with us. The largest economy in the world, which is that of the USA, is already feeling the impact of society 5.0. Over the period between 1990 and 2007, the US manufacturing sector lost 670,000 jobs as a result of automation [9], and the picture looks bleak on a global scale as more than 6 million jobs have been lost to industrial robots and automation technologies, and as we approach society 5.0 realities, the picture of human-based jobs looks bleaker in the manufacturing and agricultural sectors. It is estimated that 73 million jobs are at risk of being automated in the next 5–10 years [10]. In the US agricultural sector and between 1990 and now, 41% of Americans were farmers, and today that number is around 2% [9] as smart agriculture takes effect and the traditional one declines more in society 5.0. It is important to note that automation, one of the defining features of society 5.0 that will grow exponentially, includes capital, software, smart machinery, robots and artificial intelligences (AI), and its impact is often invisible and requires astute leadership. It is, however, a misnomer and a false narrative to assume that automation and digitisation technologies only lead to job losses. New technologies disrupt traditional work patterns but create new opportunities for new kinds of work and new roles for humans in the workplace. For instance, in the UK, research on impact of new technologies on the work market shows that by 2037, new technologies will create more work than it sheds. It is estimated that the healthcare sector will create more than 1 million jobs and other sectors with growth prospects include law, accounting, advertising, cybersecurity, robot technicians and education if it invests now on developing fusion skills (human-machine capabilities) via multiple platforms and accessing requisite expertise across the globe through optimal use of new technologies. These issues form a backdrop of the study that was undertaken within the university setting on teasing out the human-machine collaborations for cocreating new value propositions and possibly compelling a rethink of how universities should prepare and ready themselves for the inevitabilities and disruptions of society 5.0 (**Figure 2**).

Figure 2.
Societal evolutions (adopted from: 2017 Conference Proceedings on Future Services and Societal Systems in Society 5.0).

2.2 The creative potential of intelligent technologies

The ubiquity and power of computational capabilities increased substantially in information society 4.0 and are set to exponentially grow in the digital society 5.0 albeit in ways never imagined before. Big data analysis and interpretation by intelligent technologies, internet of things, robotics and other new technologies will, in the society 5.0, exceed human capabilities and generate new value propositions in areas of mobility, agriculture, health, energy and all aspects of human needs. For instance, diverse data from automobiles, weather forecasts, traffic, accommodations, tourist attractions and personal preferences would be recombined and reconfigured by intelligent technologies in ways that benefit the tourism industry. Mobility of the elderly and physically impaired will be substantially improved with advanced and smart wheelchairs. We will, in society 5.0, talk about smart manufacturing that employs intelligent technologies for interplant coordination that produce greater efficiencies that were never imagined before and smart healthcare that use intelligent devices in storing, retrieving and interpreting physical and medical data as well as use drones to provide on-time delivery of medications. New value creations will even reach the agriculture sector resulting in automated tractors, automated water management and self-driving delivery cars.

These new value creation opportunities would not have been possible without shifts and advances in technological capabilities. In the past, smart machines required that they be programmed and reprogrammed in order to perform specific tasks. This is what I call operating within quiescent algorithmic frameworks which, in the past, reduced machines to complimentary but generally passive tools. More than two decades ago, advances in technologies offered new possibilities in the interface between humans and machines. Technologies, especially computer technologies, had so advanced as to allow them to contribute in aiding cognitive processing, anchor intellectual performance and enrich human intellect. The shift was on effects and capabilities that technologies had on humans and moved from effects of technology to effects with and of a technology. Salomon et al. [11] define this distinction thus 'effects with technology occur when people work in partnership with machines, whereas effects of technology occur when such a partnership with machines have subsequent cognitive spin-off effects for humans working away from machines'. These crucial and early scholarly rumblings on the relationship between machines and humans focused largely on the implications of such technological advances on human cognition with some scholars arguing that this new partnership between humans and smart technologies would lead to reexamination of prevailing conceptions of intelligence and ability [11–13]. The questions revolved around intellectual property ownership in terms of whether the intellectual benefits that accrue from the human-smart technologies collaborations should be attributed to humans or whether they must be acknowledged as joint ownership with the status of smart technologies ownership posing a complex conundrum. This conundrum was, however, not new especially in education and human skilling as Pea [14] and Papert [15] raised the issue almost three decades ago in relation to ordinary and scientific calculators' role in human thinking and learning processes especially the resultant cognitive residue attribution. There was going to be an inevitable attribution effect and opened a research gap on the relationship between humans and intelligent technologies. With the advent of expanded intelligent technologies which now includes AI capabilities, the conundrum would be even more pronounced given the huge resource commitment that comes with the use of AI capabilities. This conundrum would extend to the human-machine collaborations for cocreation of value with the questions arising as to who becomes the owner of the innovative idea or new products. This matter is relevant to this chapter because human-machine partnerships for value cocreation include issues of not only intellectual property rights but also the commercialization of the generated creative ideas. For instance, within the university and developing countries context, these AI capabilities will most likely be accessed via universities by the share weight of their costs and opportunities to use these human-machine collaborations, for value cocreation could only happen in these spaces. The question of the ownership of the generated creative idea and its commercialization would naturally develop into a conflict and clashes with established cultures in universities and developing countries. In developed countries such as in Scandinavia, such ownership of new ideas and accruing commercialization benefits go to the generator of the innovation as clearly articulated in their national innovation strategies [6, 16, 17]. Even when that is the case, data collected in selected Scandinavian universities show that the university cultures have ensured general marginalisation of such practices. Universities generally play a minimal role in such activities because very little incentives accrue to the university as all costs of the innovation centres, while located within universities, are met by the government including staff salaries, office space and the whole administrative shebang.

Partnerships between humans and machines would become even more acute when humans realise that automation poses a threat to their well-being and unless clear protocols of use in the production system and innovation are clarified. Scholarly work has been done on the trust levels between humans and machines which demonstrates that lack of clarity on the roles of intelligent technologies in productivity and performance could be counterproductive. It is not difficult to discern that the following five benefits will accrue to companies and industries that leverage intelligent technologies capabilities that include AI. These benefits are increased flexibility of the work, speed of task completion, scale of productivity, and quick and superior decision-making processes based on big data interpretations that smart machines make possible. The companies, according to Xu and Dudek [18], that harness the collaborative and combined intelligence capabilities of both humans and smart machines are likely to be highly effective and competitive. According to Xu and Dudek [18], smart machines expand human abilities in three ways through amplifying humans' cognitive strengths, automating routine tasks and freeing humans to focus on innovation and other tasks the smart machines cannot perform. However, they argue that in order to optimise human-machine collaborations and increase trust between humans and machines, humans ought to perform three tasks such as training machines to perform certain tasks, explain the outcomes of those tasks and ensure the sustainability of machines in ways that ensure that machines do not harm humans in anyway. Other studies on trust issues between humans and machines focus on experimentations and simulations to measure how trust impact overall tasks completions and performance in organisations that employ human-machine collaborations [5, 19, 20]. Other studies on collaborations have signified the role of trust in team formation and development. These studies are equally important in human-machine collaborations as they go into the heart of organizational culture and how it could be affected by human-machine collaborations. The way human-machine collaborations could affect organizational culture and illuminate factors such as trust or mistrust of technological advances was measured in this study through the use of qualitative and quantitative measures. Similar to Xu and Dudek [18] observation and my own study that is reported in this chapter, trust studies on human-machine collaborations highlight the reality that organisational culture could torpedo the good intentions of human-machine partnerships. While studies that investigate trust relations between human-machine interactions focus on achievement of optimal performance by paying attention to delivering suitable and practical measures of trust variables that can be harnessed for high performance, a modicum of attention is put on the role of organisational culture in ensuring the successful use of human-machine collaborations. Freedy et al. [5] study on trust variables regarding human-machine collaborations developed and experimentally tested trust variables within the mixed initiative team performance assessment system (MITPAS) using simulations. The testing was based on the degree to which the levels of robot autonomy as well as its adaptive automation enhance soldiers' teleoperation and limit the continued use of such human-based task within the framework of trust. In other words, how far should technology go in terms of automating this human function without alienating humans which could potentially affect task accomplishment and the success of the mission. The results show that while teleoperations could be fully automated, critical performance factors of human teams such as information exchange gleaned from intelligence, coordinated communication, expected soldier behaviours in such missions and team leadership remain central to the successful mission accomplishment. Although automation via robots took away aspects of human tasks in a mission, it accentuated other aspects of human abilities as harnessed through teams such as the degree of predictability of each stage of the mission, leadership and risk assessment. This way, the findings show, the human-machine collaboration became effective.

When applied within the creative design where value creation becomes key, Pu and Lalanne [21] identify complex cognitive processes, artistic intuition and a rich repertory of knowledge and experiences as exclusive domains of humans that make exploration of new possibilities probable through targeting current imperfections in the world. Humans will therefore, according to the authors, play the role of framing the exploration, while intelligent technologies will provide big data analysis and processing. Their study focused on developing an architectural method of harnessing human-machine partnering for designs that target newness or higher designs of existing things. The results show that semi-automation and human collaboration are likely to harness the capabilities of human = machine collaborations. These conceptions of human-machine collaborations occurred at the time when intelligent technologies were still moving into the deep learning mode. Currently, these machines are capable of deep learning and thus can adapt to different tasks with little or no human effort. It is this ability of smart machines to adapt and learn deeply that has opened possibilities for these technologies to attempt generating creative ideas, concepts or models. As a result of the confluence of three main factors, the AI capabilities have been profoundly enhanced to a point of considering them for providing creative solutions. The first factor involves swathes of big data that get filtered and analysed in ways that can lead to reorganisation, recombination and reinterpretation of data, concepts and ideas such that unique, unexpected ideas or patterns could emerge heuristically. However, the current deep learning models of smart machines rely on massive datasets that must still be labelled by humans so that the system could understand what each piece of data represents. This is what is called supervised learning that depends on humans for data labelling which is quite tedious and laborious. The data labelling can also open itself to human bias and thus compromise the quality of such learning. If deep learning models are going to be more efficient in creating value and generating useful ideas, then these models are going to require scaling-up across complex and highly diversified tasks and shift towards small datasets. For smart machines to generate real value then attempts will be required to:

- Find ways of training systems to function on small datasets.

- Develop means for these systems to achieve symbolic reasoning

- Develop capabilities that allow these systems to learn in an unsupervised manner, that is, be able to use raw, unlabelled data to generate real value with little or no human effort. There are currently important pointers towards teaching systems to reason albeit in narrow applications such as in self-driving cars. There is still a lot of work yet to be done to achieve system's deep reasoning.

The second variable in the AI growth equation entails the graphic processing units (GPUs) which allows for complex computations.

The third of such factors relates to the re-emergence of old AI computation model that makes deep learning possible. However, as indicated earlier, more effort will be required to push towards unsupervised learning, and AI computation is insufficient as new algorithms and possibly even more advanced hardware will be necessary to grow AI into deep reasoning spaces.

With considerable effort, the combined capabilities of data, GPUs and deep learning could facilitate greater AI growth and efficiency in creating value and constant generation of useful ideas that can be translated into tangible results. Current machine capabilities require human effort to function optimally and are also still limited in terms of executing common-sense activities and improvising in order to adapt to real-life complexities. This state of affairs allow for human-machine collaborations in generation of useful ideas and translating them into real value. In summing up this sub-section, it is important to point out that there is a tendency to limit the meaning of creativity to disrupting established patterns through reorganising, recombining and reinterpreting data, ideas and concept. While these issues form part of creativity, creativity is more than just the generation of unique or unexpected ideas. When those ideas, despite their statistical rarity, do not lead to usefulness or human conveniences (social impact) then such ideas lack proper salience and cannot lead to real value.

2.3 The collaborative potential of human-machine partnership in value cocreation

Until such time that machine learning could be unsupervised such that these systems could use raw, unlabelled small data to generate reasoning capabilities that allow machines to function optimally across broader swath of applications and in real, complex situations using even common-sense capabilities, then human-machine collaborations will become the order of the day in value cocreation over the next two to three decades. In this sub-section, I attempt to look at possible areas of these human-machine collaborations. I have already pointed to those areas of collaboration and only seek to make them more logical and clearer. Areas for possible human-machine collaborations include:

- Use of machines to source, analyse and interpret large volumes of data which humans use to resolve real, protracted problems.

- Humans adapt unique ideas or concepts generated by smart machines to real situations to create real value.

- Machines identify previously invisible inefficiencies through sensors in complex industrial and logical systems, and humans develop means of eliminating these inefficiencies.

- Digital simulations allow for the design and testing of virtual prototypes which humans can refine and adapt in order to create real value.

The capabilities of smart machines to analyse, interpret, reorganise, recombine and reinterpret data allow humans to improve existing products and services so as to increase their salience and efficiency and thus both cocreate real value. These human-machine collaborative capabilities also provide for the development of products and services that are disruptive of existing order of things.

3. Human-machine supercreativity in complex university settings

Universities have traditionally been designed to conduct research and teach. Overtime, universities have become implicated in the resolution of protracted societal problems but have also been experiencing high-level and high-stakes evaluations in the form of university rankings and strategic planning which were attempting to alter the very plinth of what a university is meant to be so they could function as quasi-businesses. In the South African context, universities have been given an added burden of resolving historical inequality and poverty. These profound and sustained strategic onslaughts on the university have, however, failed to fundamentally change the culture of university as academic autonomy and professional identities remain deeply ingrained. This issue demonstrates that change strategy alone is not enough to change cultures and mindset. There is a need for something more than a change strategy to affect mindset shift and significantly change a culture. As Peter Trucker once stated 'culture eats strategy for lunch'. At the heart of this quote is the need to develop a deeper understanding of organisational culture and a sociocultural analysis which becomes crucial in trying to understand how change can be effected in any organisation. Given that creativity has had a difficult relationship with faculty, curriculum and pedagogy [1] and technology use within universities has been criticised for its undertheorisation and fetishistic implementation [1], supercreativity, as others prefer to call the human-machine collaboration to cocreate new or improved value, would find a generally hostile university environment. Adapting the model developed by Daugherty and Wilson called MELDS, and incorporating aspects of a sociocultural perspective, I attempt to better understand the conditions under which supercreativity could survive and thrive within a university setting.

Mindset (*Meds*): Universities are large complex systems that have developed certain entrenched social processes that translate into deep-seated cultures. These social processes and university cultures privilege certain mindsets and displace the others. Most universities subscribe to the notion of *Magna Charta Universitatum* that European universities have formalised in a document. The charter recognises and makes sacrosanct academic freedom and formation of professional identities. These identities form over time and are often driven by a strong scholarship and values. Some of the key academic values that shape cultures of universities subsume openness to ideas and multiple if not opposing perspectives, deep awareness of own beliefs and their limitations, a non-judgemental attitude that makes academics to be slow to judge and wait for evidence and outcomes of critical analysis, a cognitive flexibility that remains open to new possibilities as well as adaptability to newness. This academic mindset allows universities to be open systems that are presumably malleable to newness, but as Becher and Trowler states in *Academic Tribes and Territories* [22], professional identities can lead to narrowness, group myopia and defence in ways that could make universities inimical to external change initiatives. It is particularly important to appeal to the malleable aspect of the academic mindset and that requires working within the framework academics better understand which is that of research and rigorous theorisation. Part of what posed resistance to technology by academics was its enactment in technocratic ways that insidiously encroached on their academic practices and professional identities [21]. As a way of negotiating an academic space for supercreativity, there is a need to work on the mindset of academics through their own research and theorisation framework. In the next sub-section, I provide and elaborate on this framework as a way of providing a model for changing academic mindsets.

Experimentation (*mELds*): If universities are to adapt to the realities of society 5.0, then they need to reimagine and rework its entire university plinth (strategy, PQM, curriculum, research, pedagogy, community engagement) around artificial intelligence (AI) technologies, automate repetitive lecture sessions based on known knowledge and experiments and access expertise throughout the globe in real time using advanced technologies. This adaptation to the disruptions of traditional university plinth would require reimagining the entire university business. The new university plinth could involve virtual lecturing (lecture sessions), on-time access to expertise across the globe, new modules around human-machine collaborations, and super-creativity delivered on an international platform. This international platform could use multiple accreditation mechanisms that enhance students brand (nothing wrong with a certificate that bears emblems of more than one knowledge institution preferably university-university, university-industry or university-specialised colleges accreditations). Joint student-staff research projects on supercreativity, innovation that leverages digital simulations and supercreativity-driven entrepreneurship using multiple platforms and accessing expertise globally will become normal in society 5.0. These are hugely experimentation precincts and they require urgent adoption. However, their adoption needs to be done in ways that do not alienate academics through undermining their academic autonomy; rather a deep commitment to incentive schemes that encourage change processes in research, teaching and curriculum would most likely nudge academics to realities of society 5.0. When Research Directorates incentive grants favour joint research undertaken with students on supercreativity, innovation based on digital simulations and supercreativity-based entrepreneurship, then chances of success increase and traditional identities based on group loyalties could exponentially vitiate. When teaching grants favour the use of virtual learning, access to expertise on a global scale and in all sectors of society through the use of technologies as well as joint research projects with students, commerce, industry, retail and local communities, then positive adoption could occur.

Leadership (*meLds*): University leadership has a responsibility to prepare universities for the next wave of new technologies that will alter the business of universities in very extraordinary ways in the next 5–25 years. There is an urgent need to revisit all university policies and align them to the realities of society 5.0 so universities could help communities of commerce, industry, retail, politics and ordinary local communities to adapt to society 5.0 realities or risk irrelevance which is worse than death. University leadership needs to change the entire university business plinth as expounded earlier and rally it around the joint capabilities of new intelligent technologies and human ingenuity. The time to craft a new university strategy around AI and other new technologies as well as around human ingenuity is now. Universities that remain stuck to traditional modes and business plinth may need to learn lessons of the manufacturing sector and realise that education and work will need to be reimagined in the age of society 5.0. The study that is reported in this chapter makes an extremely modest contribution to that debate. In fact, it is only scratching the surface but provides a starting point to initiate a new narrative within a university setting, one that takes the sociocultural realities of a university into account in matters of crafting smart strategies for the university. Smart strategies will have to shift focus away from traditional task-oriented operations towards investing heavily in human-machine collaborations and activities of supercreativity.

Data (*melDs*): Universities have always been driven by big data and have historically struggled to manage it. With new technologies such as Hadoop, storing big data has become quite a cinch. The critical issue and of relevance to this chapter is what to do with these big nuggets of textual and numerical data sourced in multiple ways and through all types of formats including sensors, RFID tags and smart monitoring most of which are either structured or unstructured. There is a need to develop some form of organising these big data. This can be organised in terms of the time or period when such big data is available which is termed 'periodic peaks'. The organising of such data could also be done in terms of relevance to a particular aspect of university business (strategy, PQM, curriculum, pedagogy, registration and censors, security including cybersecurity) and more importantly on how it helps universities to drive supercreativity, smart innovation and technopreneurship. A smart scoping review of these big data could make these data relevant to creativity, innovation and entrepreneurship through cleansing, connecting and correlating such data with cocreation of new or improved value. A smart scoping review combines the human-machine capabilities for accessing stored data, cleansing, connecting and correlating these data with value creation.

Skills (*meldS*): Society 5.0 renders traditional skills inadequate but creates new opportunities for fusion skills. While the concept of fusion skills is relatively new especially when used within the university context and requires better understanding so it could be integrated into courses, graduate attributes and form part of core curricula. Fusion skills serve as a collective concept for the effects of digital disruption, that is, these kinds of skills have the capability to fundamentally alter workflows, business models and relationships of value creation such as, in the university context, strategy, PQM, curriculum, pedagogy as well as research and scholarship. For the purpose of this chapter, fusion skills are understood as creative skillsets that support:

- Smart team formation and leveraging of human-machine capabilities to create new or improved value propositions

- Development of smart innovation and technopreneurship

- Broad and smart collaborations that disrupt traditional modes of partnerships in the classroom that is based on in-house expertise towards smart collaborations with experts all over the globe and machine-based expertise (Siri, Bixby, Google Assistant and videoconferencing to state the easy-to-access intelligent technologies)

4. The research design

4.1 Context and purpose of study

This study was undertaken within two different geographical contexts—Scandinavia and South Africa—in order to make a comparative case of how creativity and innovation are handled in these spaces. As earlier stated, universities feel the urge to protect academic autonomy and professional identities, and if these two factors are ignored, then mindset shifts towards society 5.0 could be significantly delayed. In Scandinavia, attempts are made to drive creativity and innovation from the national government level through setting their agenda and strong financing, yet these activities remain on the margins of the core university activities because the National Innovation Strategy did not take into account the sociocultural aspects of the universities. Given that society 5.0 somehow demands that universities ought to embrace and leverage more fervently and passionately the benefits of combined capabilities of intelligent technologies as made possible by artificial intelligence (AI) advances and human ingenuity, then a more measured approach, that is, one that accounts for the entrenched institutional culture is most likely to help universities to ease into society 5.0. South African universities have an added burden of resolving social ills of poverty, unemployment and inequality, yet they have mostly and obdurately sought to emulate strategies, PQMs, curricula, pedagogy and research of developed countries as they chase the mirage of top rankings. The very notion that universities are ranked on the basis of research outputs with inadequate additional indicators on impact of such research on society and its future prospects is problematic. These extra indicators in league tables could help nudge universities into society 5.0. In both contexts, there is a strong call for universities to drive creativity and innovation, yet these activities remain largely outside the core university plinth. Annual reports of these universities paint a clearer picture of this general marginalisation. The purpose of the study was thus to understand better the conditions under which those that drive innovation and entrepreneurship in universities operate and how supercreativity could possibly negotiate a space in these complex university spaces and help drag universities into society 5.0.

4.2 Sampling and selection

Universities: Five Scandinavian universities were selected via an exponential non-discriminatory snowballing technique. I linked up with my network in one of the Swedish universities who arranged that I become a guest researcher in their Centre for Engineering Education for 3 months. He also arranged the first interview with the Deputy-Dean for Innovation and Collaborations who then pointed me to the Directors in Innovation Hubs and Centres for Entrepreneurship. These Directors, in turn, suggested names of Directors of other universities. I was able to interview 13 of these Directors from five different Scandinavian universities.

The three South African universities were selected on the basis that they were considered as the top three innovative universities in South Africa. This ranking was done by and is available in the 2017 Clarivate Analytics Report. All these three universities are research-intensive. The Directors of Innovation Hubs, Technology Transfer units or similar units dealing with innovation within these universities were interviewed. All in all, 6 Directors were interviewed totalling 18 research participants.

Digital artificial intelligence (AI) assistant tools: Given that the main purpose of the experiment was to better understand the conditions under which humans and machines could interact and possibly collaborate in the creation of new value propositions, I sought a more advanced but simple digital AI assistant tool that is easily available and easy to use. The digital AI tool could be available on any computer or mobile devices. Three such latest and smartest AI tools that facilitate human-machine interactions are Google Assistant, Apple Siri and Samsung Bixby. The Google Assistant has proved to be the most advanced tool in this area of technology. It is capable of:

- Showing photos and diagrams that are taken within few weeks and within specific locations. This capability can facilitate human-machine collaboration in generation of ideas especially when baseline graphic information is required to trigger idea generation.

- Providing instance (and contextual) answers from the web and is capable of responding more specifically to most questions posed to it. This ability comes handy in terms of saving time for humans in searching for answers in huge swathes of information. It is a technological ability that could assist humans in identifying different categories of information and ideas and help with sound judgement. It also helps humans on scoping reviews of existing ideas, concepts, products and services given that creativity is about finding ideas and concepts with statistical rarity.

- Developing a memory of information and knowledge that you have previously searched. It makes it possible to ask follow-up questions and receive sensible responses.

- Reading poetry, telling a joke and translating foreign phrases. The activity of generating new or improved ideas requires multiple perspectives and combinations, recombinations and reorganisation as well as reinterpretation of information, ideas, concepts, art and so on and in whatever language as such this technological capability brings these possibilities to the fore.

- Handling complete conversations with its users, and its protocols and heuristics are open to third party developers which allows for own application which can be deployed to the Google Assistant across the globe and thus making collaboration on such a scale possible. It can thus be used to create diverse teams that can collaborate on the same Google Assistant mock-ups.

- Collecting feedback and comments on collaborated creative designs.
  Its Botsociety API allows changes in the design and multiple iterations such that a design could be refined and be ready for prototyping via digital simulations.

Based on these benefits, Google Assistant was preferred and selected over Siri and Bixby in the experiment.

4.3 Research methods

4.3.1 Interviews

Eighteen Directors of innovation hubs and entrepreneurship centres from Scandinavian universities and three from South African universities were interviewed on:

- Situatedness of their entities within the university, that is, whether they formed part of the strategic core of the university or remained on the margins

- Whether critical and creative thought was explicitly taught within the core university curriculum or in their entities

- The state of readiness for their entities and universities to embrace artificial intelligence (AI) capabilities and contribute in shaping society 5.0 and its 15 forces of disruption [5] and factors inimical to university or entity readiness

Students that participated in the experiment were also interviewed with focus on:

1. Their expectation on interacting with Google Assistant and whether they have interacted with any of these AI technologies before such as Siri, Bixby or any advanced intelligent technologies

2. How they were coping with interacting with Google Assistant (ease of use, confidence, helpfulness in finding answers, reliability of answers, what can be done to optimise the interaction) during and after the experiment

4.3.2 Quasi-experimentation

Four teams of mostly advanced undergraduate students were involved in this project pulled from a database of students who have already submitted their innovation projects to the university for possible assistance. Projects included the use of waste to produce electricity and web application development for selling second-hand books, an application for Smart Logistics. Teams had a simple task of using Google Assistant to scope the statistical rarity of their project idea, that is, whether no or very few people or businesses have already set up such a product or service. There had to be clear evidence of such statistical rarity. They also had to be clear about the need they are creating and attempting to meet and use Google Assistant to filter and analyse multiple nuggets of information pulled from Google Assistant. Google Assistant is capable of building a memory and history of number of times visited on a similar topic, periodic peaks as well as trajectory and nature of visits. Teams also had to demonstrate how Google Assistant helped them shape their approach in creating and meeting a need including competitors (statistical rarity of idea/approach) and possible benefits that will accrue to the customers/ target market. Observation of teams was done with two research assistants and we compared notes. These research assistants are postgraduate students in IT and programming. They helped retrieve evidence on the interaction of students with Google Assistant.

5. Findings and explanations

The Scandinavian Directors indicated that governments mainly drove innovation and entrepreneurship within universities through generous funding that includes fully furnished offices, salaries and small seed-funds. They also confirmed that critical and creative thinking were not explicitly taught within the core university curriculum and even within their units. Centres for Entrepreneurship offered both contact and online formal entrepreneurship programmes up to doctoral degree but their undergraduate entrepreneurship programmes have tended to struggle for space in faculties:

'some of our entrepreneurship programmes tend to be removed in preference of more traditional courses...but we keep trying to secure room for our programmes'.

There is a general acceptance of the digital tools mainly as quiescent platforms for online offerings, desktop research and as part of university operations:

'we have really not started to appreciate the huge potential of AI in entrepreneurship as an ally and to come to your question, we have not even started to explore the human-machine collaboration in driving creativity and innovation'.

The Directors also share the view that if creativity is generally marginalised on the core undergraduate curriculum, then human-machine creativity may struggle even more to find space. These Directors also indicated that Swedish universities are co-signatories of the *Magna Charta Universitatum* that defends academic freedom, and thus external change efforts may struggle to gain traction under these entrenched university cultures. Innovation Hubs tend to mostly use the NABC model to determine the ideas pitch and provide little training in terms of generation of novel ideas. In South Africa, the positioning of innovation units similar to Scandinavia remains generally outside the core university units and serves as support structures rather than as core academic activity. Entrepreneurship is mostly located in Business Schools of these three South African universities.

The results of the experiment that was undertaken with students, while preliminary and quite precarious, suggest the following team formation framework as also extrapolated from Costa and McConnell study [4]:

Emerging contours of smart team formation:

1. Pre-connectivity

There is a strong view coming from the research participants via interviews that they needed to be properly prepared for the activity in terms of:

- Developing a common understanding as human teams prior to engaging with Google Assistant. The main challenge here was that teams were formed in terms of their diversity, that is, in relation to the courses they were doing rather than on the projects they were currently running. For example, a team would consist of advanced engineering undergraduate student, a computer science student, an HR student and a humanities student. Only two teams were kept homogeneous and with their current project. The students believe developing a common ground on what to explore as a new or improved idea while trying to harness diverse knowledge bases require more time. There are just too many variables to manage, and this is seen as counterproductive from the perspectives of the research participants, 'we spent more time arguing over what our project should involves (sic) and how we could use Google Assistant to help us'. While this is seen as a constraint, it is equally an important aspect of becoming creative, and while it was a major source of frustration, it demonstrated the difficulty research participants have in shifting their mindsets that was the primary purpose of the experiment. The homogeneous teams seemed to have already overcome some of these initial team challenges.

- Most heterogeneous teams failed to go through the first stage of the experiment, that is, agreeing on the project. Two of the teams were from engineering, and we kept it as intact because they were already working on some innovation projects that focused on turning organic waste into energy. The projects of these two teams had already advanced to how the waste bins in restaurants and hotels could be developed to become the first stage of transforming waste, that is, mixing this waste and how urine could be harnessed to generate energy. Access to Google Assistant helped them gain knowledge such as waste mixing for energy yield which takes almost 30 days to be ready for the next stage of transformation, and Google Assistant also pointed the team to some relevant videos.

2. Connecting/connectivity

There are obvious challenges when teams attempt to link up with intelligent technologies such as Google Assistant. These challenges appear to develop into a typology of apprehension, doubt and cynicism when teams have not resolved what their project is about and how the intelligent technologies could help the team to shape the project. Teams that have a clear project tend to embrace the interaction with intelligent technologies better than those with a vague project and demonstrate less apprehension, less doubt about the efficiency of the team-Google Assistant interactions. Given that teams actually connected with Google Assistant in computer centres that all students used meant that each team member would have to use earphones so they could not disturb other students. There was no attempt, at this stage, to develop virtual teams that could enable cross interaction between human teams and human-machines teams within the digital space which meant that human-machine interaction occurred at an individual level. Team members then met to share information generated via interactions with Google Assistant. This led to some early superficial learning, more like sharing notes. Team members still had to agree on which information to pursue further with Google Assistant. Given the limited time I had for this experiment and indeed the experimentation is ongoing, the next stages of team development are really hypothetical and will still undergo rigorous experimentation including the identified preliminary stages of team development. My informed conjecture is that beyond the *connectivity* stage, *early superficial learning* will follow.

3. Early superficial learning

Once teams recognise the value of intelligent technologies such as Google Assistant in their projects, an exploration of what such smart machines can offer tended to follow. At this stage, learning is more focused on testing the potential and limits of the smart machine. This learning is superficial because it does not contribute directly to resolving issues in the project. Few of our research participants have not been actively using any of these intelligent technologies which might explain this exploration. There is a need to determine whether this stage may not be redundant under conditions where students have a regular use of Siri, Bixby and Google Assistant. The additional condition could be to determine the level of proficiency in using these technologies. Those research participants that have gone beyond level 1 of these technologies would most likely have a better use of these technologies than those who are using them for the first time. More experimentation will provide evidence of whether this stage is necessary or can be eliminated.

4. Intense interactivity

Following from the previous stage, the degree of interaction with Google Assistant increased substantially once its potential benefits in helping teams to work on their projects increased. As stated earlier, research participants who have beyond level 1 proficiency in working with these technologies would most likely show intense interaction with these technologies to a point where learning goes beyond understanding how the technology works to being able to interact and possibly even collaborate with it as efforts of cocreation of value increase. There is also a need to conduct a rigorous experimentation to determine whether this stage can be retained. There are strong indications that this stage can survive the rigour of research.

5. Maturing

Similar to the norming stage of Tuckman's Stages of Team Development, this stage appeared to focus teams towards the project, and the specific pieces of information and knowledge that teams required from Google Assistant tended to be more targeted to specific aspects of the project. For teams that had no clear project, this stage tended to narrow down areas that might be pursued as possible projects. For teams that started off with a clear project, this stage deals with pieces of information and knowledge that progress resolution of some aspects of the project. It is also important to note that proficiency in use of these technologies provides a basis of how teams mature into real interactions with intelligent technologies as allies in creative problem-solving.

6. Deep learning

The human-machine collaboration will work even better when intelligent technologies move away from hard-coded knowledge and can extract patterns from raw data which means functioning in an unsupervised way. This is what is called machine-learning capability because it allows for tackling problems that entail knowledge of the real world which is informal, intuitive and subjective. Creative problem-solving goes beyond formal knowledge (known, established) and includes intersubjective knowledge that can be contextual and unique to certain people. Deep learning would require intelligent machines that can transform such input data that can be esoteric and informal into a slightly more abstract and composite representation in ways that could lead to the development of concepts hierarchies. Given that humans rely mostly on informal and intersubjective knowledge in problem-solving, the point of deep learning with smart machines would most likely occur at the intersection where smart machines can reason about statements in the informal, subjective language as humans bring their own informal knowledge into the equation. This will be the point where humans and smart machines generate intersubjective knowledge that allows for reimagination, which is a crucial element of creativity. Currently, smart machines can reason using logical inference rules or on the basis of the knowledge base approach which relies on formal knowledge; hence such learning is considered superficial because it is based on known, established knowledge. Deep learning, as an important stage in team development, would be achieved and observed, I posit, when the human-machine collaboration leads to reimagination. Value is often cocreated when things are reimagined. This is probably the most important stage of human-machine team development. As AI capabilities develop to make it possible for smart machines to function unsupervised, that is, on the basis of processing raw data and in similar fashion as humans who rely on informal, subjective knowledge and knowledge developed, over time, with others in particular contexts (intersubjective) to resolve problems, then deep learning that lead to creativity will be possible. Creativity is not merely about creating concepts hierarchies, frameworks and models for understanding reality. It is not also about making some ontological commitments rather is about reimagining and altering naturalistic and authentic contexts. It is about trying out things through multiple iterations, testing and refining. It is even about defying logic as its primary purpose is to seek pragmatic solutions to real problems and impact societal practices in ways that advance human conveniences. It requires smart machines with deep learning capabilities not as currently understood but as yet to be imagined.

7. Resolution

Given that the possibilities of a real deep learning between humans and smart machines remain constraint, this stage of team development remains imagined.

6. Recommendations and future direction of research

Given that university cultures remain rooted in practices and activities that are task-oriented and output-driven, investment on human and machine thinking would remain a major challenge. This challenge is exacerbated by the general marginalisation of creativity in the university plinth. It is thus suggested that more research be conducted which illuminate the potential benefits of mainstreaming human-human and human-machine creativity. More experiments with more advanced intelligent technologies would help shape the team development stages suggested in this chapter. The following areas of research are worthy of consideration:

1. More research on university cultures and their relationship with the development of staff and student creativity within the framework of human - machine collaborations

2. University management mindset shift towards AI and appreciating the future realities of society 5.0

3. More experiments to clarify and possibly refine the human-machine team formation stages

4. University investment on advanced IT and AI

Acknowledgements

The role and contribution of the Research Directorate at Vaal University of Technology particularly Dr. Speech Nelana and Ms. Chantelle Sonnekus in funding my Scandinavian research visit and pay for this platform are truly appreciated. The author would like to thank Ms. Gape Motswana in the Office of the Vice-Chancellor and Principal, Professor Gordon Zide, for both adding the magic touch to this scholarly journey.

Author details

Teboho Pitso
Vaal University of Technology, Vanderbijlpark, South Africa

*Address all correspondence to: biki@vut.ac.za

References

[1] Torgilsson P. A critical reflection on the hegemony of technology and possibilities of including ethics in public consumption [Master's degree dissertation]. Lund, Sweden: Lund University; 2015

[2] Kuzmin O, Pyrog O, Melnik L. Transformation of development model of national economies as conditions of postindustrial society. ECONTECHMOD: An International Quarterly Journal. 2014; **3**(2):41-45

[3] Tuckman B. Developmental sequence in small groups. Psychological Bulletin. 1965;**63**:384-399

[4] Crosta L, McConnell D. Challenging the traditional theorisation on group development. An international online perspective. In: The 7th International Conference on Networked Learning. 2010. pp. 3-4

[5] Freedy A, McDonough J, Freedy E, Jacobs R, Thagels S, Weltman G. A Mixed Initiative Team Performance Management Assessment System (MITPMA) for use in Training and Operational Environments. SBIR, Phase 1 Report, Constract No. N61339-04-c-0020, Perceptronics Solutions. 2004

[6] Karvonius V. National Innovation Policies in Finland. Helsinki, Finland: Ministry of Employment and the Economy Press; 2013

[7] Minter D, Storkey C. Futureproof: How to Get Ready for the Next Disruption. New York: Pearson; 2017

[8] Dweck C. Mindset: The New Psychology of Success. New York: Ballantine Books; 2007

[9] Acemoglu D, Restrepo P. Robots and Jobs: Evidence from US Labor Markets. NBER Working Paper No. w23285. 2017. Available from SSRN: https://ssrn.com

[10] Harvey L. Transitions from Higher Education to Work 2003. Available from: http://www.shu.ac.uk/research/cre/publications

[11] Salomon G, Perkins D, Globerson T. Partners in cognition: Extending human intelligence with intelligent technologies. Educational Research. 1990;**20**(3):2-9

[12] Mandinach E. Model-building and the use of computer simulation of dynamic systems. Journal of Educational Computing Research. 1989;**5**:221-243

[13] Mitchel W. Introduction: A new agenda for computer-aided design in the electronic design studio. In: Mitchell W, McColough C, editors. The Electronic Design Studio. Cambridge: MIT Press; 1990

[14] Pea R. Distributed intelligence and education. In: Paper Presented at the Annual Meeting of the Social Science Research Council on Computers and Learning, British Virgin Islands. 1989

[15] Papert S. Computer criticism vs. technocentric thinking. Educational Research. 1987;**17**(1):22-30

[16] Loof A. The Swedish Innovation Strategy. Stockholm, Sweden: Ministry of Enterprise; 2017

[17] OECD. OECD Reviews of Innovation Policy, Norway. Norway: OECD Press; 2017

[18] Xu A, Dudek G. Online Probabilistic Trust Inferences Model for Asymmetric Human Robot Collaborations. 2007. DOI: 10.1145/26964542896429

[19] Chen J, Terrence P. Effects of imperfect automation and individual differences in concurrent performance of military and robotics tasks in a

simulated multi-tasking environment. Ergonom. 2009;**52**(8):907-920

[20] Kristin E, Chen J, Szalman J, Hancock P. A meta-analysis of factors influencing the development of trust in automation: Implications for understanding autonomy in future systems. Human Factors. 2016;**58**(3): 377-400

[21] Pu P, Lalanne D. Human and Machine Collaboration in Creative Design: Technical Report. Switzerland: Ecole Polytechnique Federale de Lausanne; 1996

[22] Becher T, Trowler P. Academic Tribes and Territories. Buckingham, UK: The Society for Research into Higher Education and Open University Press; 2011

Section 3

Creativity and Human - Machine Collaborations

Chapter 6

Diginalysis: The Man-Machine Collaboration in Music Analysis

Ikenna Emmanuel Onwuegbuna

Abstract

The digital technology of the twenty-first century has put man and machine in the center stage where electronic generation, production and manipulation of the musical sound are the norm. The dynamics of the century have made time more elusive and patience more diminutive. Time and patience are vital for any form of successful exercise in music analysis. The intricacies of applying logic to resolve complex musical structures, facts, propositions, and concepts into their elements demand more than technical know-how; they demand a lot of time and patience. With the continued fleeing of time and patience, mechanical accuracy in music analysis would need a full-blown computer-driven "diginalysis." However, inherent limitations of the computer in music analysis, such as decoding the composer's ideologies, necessitate human-machine collaboration. An in-depth descriptive survey has shown that this effective collaboration between man and machine will collapse time and energy by providing immediate feedback, technical accuracy and dependable results.

Keywords: music, analysis, digital, collaboration, computer, software

1. Introduction

Analysis is considered the resolution, by application of logic, of complex structures, facts, propositions and concepts into their elements. By extension, it is the tracing of things to their source and the resolution of knowledge into its original principles, the discovery of general principles underlying concrete phenomena. Music analysis, therefore, is the dissection of the musical composition to separate the component parts of the whole in order to take a proper examination of the nature, function, connotations, compatibility, complementary and unitary contributions of these components. This exercise will, among other things, offer the analyst a chance for proper appraisal of the effects of different compositional and performance techniques on the consumers of the musical product. It will also ensure personal and institutional in-depth studies of the composition. In the words of Achinivu,

> *Through analysis, the various elements of musical architecture become less technical and less dry to music students. Conversely, by their application of the knowledge they have of musical elements and concepts in the analysis of a piece of music, they obtain greater insights into and understanding of musical design and content of form.*

IntechOpen

In the recent applications of the theory of observational learning, terms such as *mastery learning*, *teaching machines*, *programmed instruction*, *computer-based training* (CBT), *computer-aided instruction* (CAI) and *audiovisual education* have found their place in the center stage of the twenty-first century educational procedures.

Sidney Leavitt Pressey had, in the 1920s, designed the first set of teaching machines, which provided immediate feedback for multiple-choice tests. In using the machine, the learners had the advantage of correcting their errors immediately. This immediate feedback system enabled the learners to work at the test items until their answers were correct. Improving on the efforts of Pressey, B. F. Skinner, in 1954—exploring the possibilities of his operant conditioning, developed his own version of teaching machine that became known as *programmed instruction*. The basis of Skinner's programming includes simple principles, namely, presentation of information in small steps called frames, immediate confirmation of the learner's response, active responding to induce sustained activity, self-pacing and dual evaluation of learner's progress by both learner and teacher [1–4].

The application of the programmed-learning theory in analyzing music in the twenty-first century, obviously, engages the computer as an inseparable aid. The elements and items for analysis are codified and, thereby, reduced to icons which are packaged in music software (programmed). The programme then becomes the model to be observed and interacted with by the analyst, in a multimedia of presentation. Sociocultural, ideological and historical issues in music—through a human and machine collaboration—can equally, and easily, be reduced into electronic forms for analysis in the same interactive manner as in musical issues [5].

2. Approaches to music analysis

In trying to dissect music, to separate the component parts of the whole in order to take a proper examination of the nature, function, connotations, compatibility, complementary and unitary contributions of these components, the scholar has already embarked on an analytical assignment that would stretch his/her studies into other disciplines than music. Such studies, whether carried out by an individual or a team, would demand the application of knowledge from at least such academic disciplines as sociology, history, anthropology, semiology, linguistics, economics and philosophy. Because of these interpretative demands, there is a need to engage with music analysis from various approaches.

2.1 Musical approach

Certain elements are globally accepted as intrinsic commonalities in the phenomenon of sound. Such elements as rhythm, pitch, timbre and duration when consciously or subconsciously manipulated distinguish the musical sound from the rest. Analyzing music along the lines of its sonic elements, exposing the inherent stylistic features, conventions and idioms is basically in the domain of systematic musicology. This approach tends to describe 'the over-all structure of a piece of music, and ... the interrelationships of its various sections. In most cases, indeed, it is the fitting of this structure into a preconceived mode' [6].

For instance, 'form', as a basic element in music, refers to the structural make-up of a musical composition. It exposes the basic shape of the composition that gives it its distinctive character. Musical form, as one of the characteristic elements of music, is the bases of the systematic and coherent arrangement of the structural design of a musical composition. Apel, therefore, expresses the fact that:

> *Music, like all art, is not a chaotic conglomeration of sounds, but...it consists of sounds arranged in orderly manner according to numerous obvious principles as well as to a still greater number of subtle and hidden relationships which evade formulation. In this meaning, form is so essential to music that it is difficult to imagine a procedure by which it could be avoided [7].*

The musical approach to analysis exposes the stylistic features of the piece, the conventions and the exceptions in the application of those features by the composer and the performers of the piece. In this approach, the analyst is trying to appreciate the composer's application of expressive variables in music—like tonality, rhythm, form, tempo, metre, timbre, intensity and texture.

2.2 Sociocultural approach

In the sociocultural approach, music is considered not just as a sonic material but also a symbolical representation of entities, deities, communities, age-grades, generations, classes, races, norms and societies. Analysis under this approach must expose and explain the determinate associations that are implied in the musical expression and the functionality of music in society.

The sociocultural issues in music—especially the 'popular' genre—are implicated more in the processes and negotiated decisions that lead to the creation and consumption of the musical product, than in the textual pronouncements that make up the lyrics of the song, those belong to the ideological angle of the piece. Other sociocultural-related issues in popular music include recording/performance contracts, copyright protection, signing on a record label, publicity, promotion, marketing, publishing, artiste-patron agreements, collaborations, public performance and broadcasting rights and hiring the services of an entertainment law attorney.

2.3 Ideological approach

Personal opinions held by individual composers and other stakeholders in the musical enterprise, expressed in the textual materials and the musical product, form the bulk of the ideological stance of the music. These opinions could be philosophical, religious, spiritual, political, interpersonal relationships and the total world-view of the composers, which are perceptible, not just in the lyrics but also in the CD sleeves, video clips, interviews, press releases, personality image of the artistes and their style of usage of metalanguage and polyglottism.

2.4 Historical approach

In the historical approach, the analyst embarks on a retrospective study of schemata of music and how they have developed over time. He/she studies the major stylistic features that characterize each particular period and relate them to parallel developments in other forms of the arts and sciences of the same period, and how each individual composer has interpreted the dominating music of his/her own time. In addition, she/he exposes the practices that marked the points of transition from one era to the different practices of another era, thereby establishing the trends that distinguish one period from another.

3. Computer-aided music analysis

The computer technology which saw its modest beginnings in the 1960s and, within a decade of its development, succeeded in turning the world into a global village, has its impact felt in music production. From the introduction and advancement of music synthesizers and other complementary devices, the once dominating analogue audio recording devices have progressively and dexterously been replaced by digital equivalents [8]. The introduction of computer technology, therefore, started a radical turning point in audio production. This turning point has finally eclipsed the analogue system of recording, giving way to the more efficient, real-time and almost real-life digital system [9–11].

An audio recording in which the raw sounds emanating from the initial sources are represented by the spacing between pulses (bits) rather than by waves, thereby making the sounds less susceptible to degradation, is known as digital recording. In digital recording, computer programmes are used to manipulate the audio data stored in the form of alphanumeric codes. This manipulation is done through mathematical processes [8, 10, 12]. The process involves 'the description of a sound waveform as sequence of numbers representing the instantaneous amplitudes of the wave over small successive intervals of time' [9]. Some of the advantages of the digital technique, according to Salt (as cited in [13]), are:

> *In digital recording systems, many of the distortions are removed because the continuously varying sound signal is transformed into a digital signal (a sequence of binary values, or a series of bits), by a process called quantizing or quantization, as soon as it is captured. This enables the stored sound data to be checked and processed so that it can, in theory, be reproduced exactly as it was recorded.*

The basic advantage of digital storage of the musical sound is the ease of processing, manipulation and analyzing of the data. This flexibility of the digital data has made it a nearly effortless task to create sound effects, enhance quality and ease editing of the recorded sound. This flexibility makes it possible for the analyst to not only engage but also interact with the digitized items. However, the challenge lies in the reversibility of such digitized items.

The creative and production processes involve computer synthesis in digital recording—starting from the generation of audio samples from analogue sources to conversion to digital equivalents through series of voltage steps, electronic means of creating, filtering and modifying sound—mediated via special interfaces such as effects boxes, tone generators, MIDI, drumulator, vocoder and keyboard sampler.

Through the use digital audio software such as Cakewalk, Cubase, Sonar, Nuendo, Adobe Audition and Fruity Loops, among others, audio projects ranging from sampling, sequencing, quantizing, voicing, boosting, compressing, mixing, recording, re-mixing, etc. are successfully delivered. Music analysis is greatly favored by the instant generation of notated music scores by these audio production music software.

In the application of the computer as the analytical tool, the musical elements are codified and, thereby, reduced to icons which are packaged in music software (programmed). The programme then becomes the model to be observed and interacted with by the analyst, in a multimedia of presentation. The reduction of the elements into electronic forms is the major duty of the computer programmers. The analyst, working with professional computer programmers who are adepts in computer programming language, reduces the issues and elements in music into icons for which the options for digitized items are only a click away.

In analyzing the musical elements of tonality, rhythm, form, tempo, metre, timbre, intensity, texture, vocal/performance techniques and orchestration, among others, the items are reduced to icons backed up with motion pictures, simulations, musical examples, sound clips, diagrams, graphs and charts, all of which are activated as soon as the right icon is clicked at. By engaging the computer programmes, any analyst can dissect a piece of music by selecting and clicking at the right icons to access and interact with the compositional rationalizations of the music composer.

Sociocultural, ideological and historical issues in music can equally, and easily, be reduced to electronic forms for analysis in the same interactive manner as in musical issues. In this multimedia formats, computer-aided music analysis encourages interactive relationships between the analyst and the models through the use of images (still and motion), animations, speeches, sounds, figures and, mostly, music. It is advantageous that the analyst can quickly access information, get immediate feedback, move at his/her own pace, monitor his/her progress, motivate him/herself and learn independently [14–17].

In this era of digital technology, the prospects of computer-aided music analysis have inspired computer programmers to create many programmes with different capabilities and limitations. Some of the programmes are the Digital Alternative Representation of the Musical Score (DARMS), Humdrum, Finale, Sibelius, Lemon and Studio 4. Others with some specialization in audio analysis include Fourier, SoundEdit, AudioSculpt, SARA and Lemur [18–20].

4. The collaboration

Sociocultural issues in music are implicated more in the processes and negotiated decisions that lead to the creation and consumption of the musical product than in the textual pronouncements that make up the lyrics of the song. Here music is considered not just as a sonic material but also a symbolical representation of entities, deities, communities, age-grades, generations, classes, races, norms and societies. Analysis must expose and explain the determinate associations that are implied in the musical expression. The functionality of music in society becomes the main focus of the analyst. Is the purpose for music-making self-fulfilling or group-fulfilling? Is it to train, to communicate, to enlighten, to worship, to praise, to heal, to supplicate, to mourn, to mock, to invoke, to curse, to defy, to survive or what? And what social events are they linked with?

Whether on a live stage or an electronic stage, one observes that the emotions expressed by music performers are not always felt by the artistes; sometimes they are feigned to create a contingent, a utilitarian or an esthetic value. The simulated emotions are constructively packaged by the producers to disguise the commercial intent, thereby succeeding in presenting the art as necessary, useful or entertaining in itself.

The stochastic nature of the foregoing makes it difficult for the computer to detect or decode the creative intent of the composers of such musical phenomena and activities. This limitation also applies to the subject matter encoded in CD sleeves, video clips, interviews, press releases, personality image of the artistes and their style of usage of metalanguage and polyglottism.

The foregoing makes the human-machine collaboration imperative. While the computer analyzes the machine-modifiable music notations, simulations, animations and icons, the rest of the variables that are largely psychological, sociological and philosophical are humanly analyzed to make up for the limitations of the machine. This model of collaboration therefore bestrides the music domain and other related disciplines including visual arts, architecture, design and film-making and editing.

5. Conclusion

The chapter has proposed the effective collaboration of human and the machine in analyzing music—especially in this twenty-first century where the computer age has expanded the frontiers of the audiovisual creativity—via the system of computer-aided music analysis.

Resources for the composition and performance of electronic music have recently been broadened considerably through the introduction and use of the Musical Instrument Digital Interface (MIDI). The MIDI, as a remarkable system, enables composers to manage quantities of complex information and allow computers, synthesizers, sound modules, drum machines and other electronic devices from many manufacturers to communicate with each other. Originally of interest only to a few so-called serious composers, today MIDI-based systems, are used to analyze and teach music, write and perform film scores, create rhythm tracks for popular music and provide music for computer games. Also with the MIDI, the numbers of ways in which the electronic synthesizer may serve composers seem limited only by the boundaries of human initiative and perception [21, 22].

Music, bestriding art and science, affects a zone where emotion intersects with processes taking place at a corporeal level and is capable of producing tactile, sensuous and involuntary reactions. The musical sound has the ability to change the emotional and physical states of people and could equally alter one in many ways, depending on the composer's manipulation of musical elements and the producer's manipulation of post-production sonic enhancements [23].

By acknowledging this protean nature of music, the chapter has identified the limitations of a single mode of analysis and therefore recommends the dual mode of man-machine collaboration in 'diginalysis'. In this effective collaboration, the computer analyzes the machine-modifiable music notations, simulations, animations and icons, while the human handles the psychological, sociological and philosophical elements of music. While the utilitarian value of this effective collaboration collapse time and energy by providing immediate feedback, technical accuracy and dependable results, the contingent will benefit other related disciplines including visual arts, architecture, design and film-making and editing.

Author details

Ikenna Emmanuel Onwuegbuna
Department of Music, University of Nigeria, Nsukka, Enugu, Nigeria

*Address all correspondence to: ikenna.onwuegbuna@unn.edu.ng

References

[1] Chauhan SS. Advanced Educational Psychology. New Delhi: Vikas; 1987

[2] Ittelson JC. Audiovisual education. In: Microsoft® Student [DVD]. Redmond, WA: Microsoft Corporation; 2009

[3] Tiemann PW, Markle SM. Teaching machines. In: Microsoft® Student [DVD]. Redmond, WA: Microsoft Corporation; 2009

[4] Achinivu AK. Teaching and understanding musical elements and concepts through analysis. Awka Journal of Research in Music and the Arts. 2003;**1**:54-68

[5] Onwuegbuna IE. Pop music analysis in the 21st century: An adaptation of the Pressey-Skinner programmed-learning theory. Awka Journal of Research in Music and the Arts. 2009;**6**:90-104

[6] Nettl B. Theory and Method in Ethnomusicology. New York: The Free Press; 1963

[7] Apel W. The Harvard Dictionary of Music. London: Heinemann; 1964

[8] Fuertes C. Computer Music. 2006. Available from http://www.pie.xtec.es [Retrieved: July 23, 2006]

[9] Moog RA. The electronic music synthesizer. In: Encyclopaedia Britannica. Ultimate Reference Suite. Chicago: Encyclopaedia Britannica; 2009

[10] Norman K. Electronic music. In: Microsoft® Student [DVD]. Redmond, WA: Microsoft Corporation; 2009

[11] Salt B. Sound recording and reproduction. In: Microsoft® Student [DVD]. Redmond, WA: Microsoft Corporation; 2009

[12] Machlis J, Forney K. The Enjoyment of Music. 7th ed. New York: W.W. Norton; 1995

[13] Onwuegbuna IE. Digitizing the analogue: The creative and economic impacts of the Nigerian audio engineer. Journal of the Association of Nigerian Musicologists. 2011;**5**:68-79

[14] Arnold DN. Computer-based training. In: Microsoft® Student [DVD]. Redmond, WA: Microsoft Corporation; 2009

[15] Kelly SN. A sociological basis for music education. International Journal of Music Education. 2002;**39**:40-49

[16] Lebler D. Student-as-master? Reflections on a learning innovation in popular music pedagogy. International Journal of Music Education. 2007;**25**(3):205-221

[17] Portowitz A, Klein PS. MISC-MUSIC: A music program to enhance cognitive processing among children with learning difficulties. International Journal of Music Education. 2007;**25**(3):259-271

[18] Brown AR. Music Education and Computers: Amplifying Musicality. New York: Routledge; 2007

[19] Gerhard D. Computer Music Analysis, Technical Report CMPT TR 97-13. Simon Fraser University, School of Computing Science; 2002

[20] Meredith D, editor. Computational Music Analysis. New York: Springer; 2016

[21] Rumsey F. MIDI Systems and Control. Toronto: Focal Press; 1994

[22] Rowe R. Interactive Music Systems. Cambridge: MIT Press; 1993

[23] Meddis R, O'Mard L. Psychophysically faithful methods for extracting pitch. In: IJCAI Workshop on Computational Auditory Scene Analysis. Montreal, Quebec; 1995. pp. 19-25

Chapter 7

The Machine-Human Collaboration in Healthcare Innovation

Neta Kela-Madar and Itai Kela

Abstract

The biopharma industry is in crisis, demonstrated by unsustainable research and development (R&D) costs. In parallel, the healthcare system suffers from skyrocketing costs, driven by the prevalence of chronic diseases and increased life expectancy. Innovative technologies have the potential to alleviate challenges both in the biopharma R&D model and in healthcare. This chapter considers how Big Data analysis based on artificial intelligence and machine learning offer opportunities to drive greater efficiency across the entire R&D value chain, enhance the quality of assets produced, and improve the time and cost to bring products to market. We also consider the unique challenges that arise with the integration of these fields into healthcare and medicine, specifically, the initially high costs when new medical and healthcare technologies are brought to the marketplace; widening socioeconomic health inequalities due to high marketplace costs; and unique methodological challenges presented by cross industry innovation, research, development, and implementation.

Keywords: artificial intelligence, healthcare, biopharma industry, personalized medicine, big data, digital transformation, machine learning, R&D, innovation

1. Introduction

The biopharma industry is facing significant challenges reflected by unsustainable research and development (R&D) costs. This challenge is seen in several ways. First, aggressive pricing pressure has led to an increase in the cost needed to bring products to market—from $1.188 billion in 2010 to a record level of $2.168 billion in 2018. A second major reason is the threat of patent expirations on numerous blockbuster drugs. As a result, biopharma companies experienced record low R&D returns in 2018—10.1% in 2010 to 1.9% in 2018, the lowest levels the industry has seen in 9 years [1].

In parallel to biopharma challenges, the healthcare system is having a crisis due to the prevalence of chronic diseases and increased life expectancy, the main causes for skyrocketing healthcare costs (in US, the health share of GDP is 18% and expected to reach 19.6% by 2014) [2]. Today, 50% of the entire US population is considered chronic patients, which accounts for 85% of the overall cost of healthcare [3]. Fortunately, the majority of chronic diseases can be prevented or delayed until significantly later stages in life due to successful medical interventions.

Today, the healthcare industry is seeing an integration of novel genetic and digital technologies that help identify and cope with the complexity of chronic diseases and their often "silent" transition from healthy status to an active disease with a late onset of symptoms. The challenge is to move medical interventions upstream to the pre-disease state, during which symptoms are cheaper and easier to treat. Significant change must be made to the current pharma R&D model, if productivity and profitability are ever to be restored and maximized. The view today is that a complete digital transformation is what is needed to achieve these goals and deliver the next generation of scientific breakthroughs.

Big Data analysis based on artificial intelligence (AI) and machine learning (ML) offer opportunities to address some of these challenges expected to drive greater efficiency across the entire R&D value chain, and eventually improve the quality of the assets produced, as well as the time and cost it takes to bring them to the market. The change is already beginning to take place. In fact, most of the big pharma companies (such as Novartis, Roche, Pfizer, Merck, AstraZeneca, GlaxoSmithKline, Sanofi, Abbvie, Bristol-Myers Squibb, Johnson & Johnson, etc.) are already on the road to taking advantage of AI innovation (healthcareweekly.com, online) as it becomes a driving force in the innovation of medicine and healthcare.

AI is a growing industry of personalized health technology, or personalized medicine, which will have tremendous effect on healthcare management. The key idea behind the technological personalization of medicine and healthcare is to capture, analyze, and utilize individual patient characteristics, such as biomarkers, then to base medical decisions on these individual characteristics rather than on population averages. Another direct application is the technological development of assisted devices that augment traditional medical practice and healthcare, such as the broad use of robotics as well as patient-worn devices ("wearables") that optimize care. This chapter reviews leading publications in these areas and outlines major advantages and also methodological and clinical weak points that need to be addressed in order for personalized medicine to realize its potential.

2. Toward personalized medicine age

Advances in technology are shifting the practice of medicine from anecdotal to data-driven. Due to this shift, improvement in screening, prediction, diagnosis, and the treatment of disease has increased the quality of medical care worldwide and cost effectively ([4]: p. 139). Personalized medicine is generally recognized as promising and advantageous in several important ways. It can improve the efficacy of medication as treatments become better matched to patients; when patients are better matched to treatments, ineffective treatments and their accompanying harmful side effects are avoided; healthcare costs are driven down as a result of better use of therapies; diseases are detected sooner or even anticipated so care is shifted from detection to prevention, thereby avoiding late-care, less effective, and more costly treatment; disease management is more effective through wearable patient technology; and clinical trials can be more accurate as patient selection becomes more precise ([5]: pp. 1-2).

Despite these apparent advantages, the technological personalization of medicine brings numerous challenges that must be addressed in order to harness its full potential. When healthcare and medical technologies first enter the marketplace, for example, they are often initially more expensive, as the companies that develop these products need to recoup high expenses from R&D. As a result, personalized health technologies are utilized first by the more affluent, driving an even larger wedge between affluent populations and marginalized ones. This serves to broaden the already wide socioeconomic gap in health inequalities in the short term ([5]: p. 2).

Solutions must be found to provide for diverse socioeconomic patient access to personalized medicine, so that its benefits reach all populations. This is especially important as marginalized and disadvantaged populations are precisely the ones least likely to access and utilize these products, but typically the very populations that would disproportionally benefit from them. Early disease diagnosis and management provided by advances in personalized medicine are especially needed in these populations and innovating for these populations is crucial in order for personalized health technology to reach its public health potential. For this, creative, strategic health initiatives must be developed that aim to lower costs while expanding access ([6]: pp. 2–4).

3. Challenges of human-machine innovation

The challenge in personalized medicine is methodological and inherent in cross-industry innovation itself—the ways in which different technologies are utilized for healthcare and medicine. While machine learning techniques can process complex and large data and provide accurate predictions based on this analysis, they are unable to provide a deeper understanding of phenomena ([6]: p. 5). In this way, Data Science and AI do not replace classical research. As a result, there remains a gap between the potential of personalized medicine and its realized application borne out as solutions that impact clinical practice.

One foreseeable way to bridge this gap is to push for a better coordinated interdisciplinary effort. Scientists, physicians, patients and their advocates, regulatory agencies, and health insurance providers need to create a healthcare system that can learn and adapt as it develops ([6]: p. 12). In short, technology is not meant to replace physicians. Rather, the idea is to provide physicians with a tool that supports their decisions based on the accurate processing, understanding, and analysis of large amounts of already available biomedical data ([6]: p. 13).

Another way to understand this difficulty is that personalized medicine is "underpinned" by convergent, cross-industry innovation. This naturally results in complexity, and uncertainty in terms of organization ([7]: p. 44). The question becomes how best to innovate given this challenge of cross-industry integration.

The two dominant forms of organizational learning aim for simplification and specialization. This is especially so in the context of uncertainty and complex integration issues that arise from innovation in an emerging cross-industry ecosystem. However, new research suggests a need to face this complexity via an adaption of a multitude of approaches, recognizing that uncertainty and risk are part and parcel of the very nature of innovation.

In this context, the management of risk might best be replaced with addressing uncertainty, understanding that in an emerging ecosystem of convergent innovation, comprehensive understanding is lacking. Approaches that embrace complexity rather than just managing it might prove more effective, specifically by adopting numerous measures to address the divergent factors in cross-industry innovation ([7]: pp. 51–52).

4. AI and digital healthcare case study: AI for cardiac patients

As a case in point, consider the impact of AI in cardiology and cardiac imaging. Machine learning and the "deep" neural networks used for this purpose hold great promise when applied to medical imaging. Improving the identification accuracy in patients at risk for cardiovascular events is critical, as well as patients who are not at risk but suffer from misdiagnosis and are given unnecessary and sometimes harmful treatments with negative side effects. The importance of improving the accuracy in detection and diagnosis is thus monumental given that cardiovascular disease is leading cause of death worldwide ([4]: p. 139).

The use of AI in cardiology has increased dramatically in the past 5 years. Machine learning algorithms now outperform many traditional algorithms, including the established risk prediction algorithm used by the American College of Cardiology (ACC)/American Heart Association (AHA), performing with a 3.6% predictive accuracy improvement over the ACC/AHA algorithm ([4]: p. 139).

Still major challenges lie ahead. Before AI can reliably be utilized by any field of medicine let alone realize its potential for cardiac patients, the neural networks necessary for its application require constant and extremely time-consuming expansion and revision. Key difficulties are (i) the extremely large amount of training data required by neural networks; (ii) the need to annotate (label) any dataset used for the training of a neural network; (iii) creating an understating of what computers learn given that the patterns and knowledge gained by a network are contained in the weights of the nodes of the network; and (iv) the risk of "overfitting" the training data when designing and training a neural network.

In other words, better efficiency of machine learning, together with improved accuracy with less training and data necessary, are all needed in order to approximate the efficiency of human learning and bring its relevance to a clinical setting.

Given these challenges, AI in cardiac CT angiography has made tremendous gains in the past 10 years, and over the next 10 years, the expectation is that we will see more AI software development and use in cardiac imaging than in the past 50 years ([4]: p. 139).

5. Decision-making tools for practitioners

A recent study revealed that one in every 71 cases from 6000 tissue samples of cancer patients across the US was misdiagnosed and up to one in five were misclassified. This same study reviewed 25 years of US malpractice claims and concluded that diagnostic errors were the cause of the most severe patient harm. According to the National Academies' Institute of Medicine, 10% of patient deaths and as much as 17% of hospital complications are a result of diagnostic errors ([8]: p. 1).

What is more, it was not primarily the physicians who were the cause of most diagnostic errors. Instead, the study found, the fault lies primarily in substandard collaboration and synthesis of information in the healthcare system as well as communication gaps, and that the healthcare system as a whole failed to effectively support the diagnostic process ([8]: p. 1).

Now let us consider the application of AI to address the need for collaboration and integration in healthcare to improve the diagnostic process. Optum, a leading company providing these solutions for the healthcare industry, developed a program called Care Coordination Platform. It processes vast amounts of data and provides a comprehensive overview of every patient's full medical history, allowing healthcare providers an immediate, complete picture of each patient. The platform suggests the most appropriate and cost-effective treatment options; identifies high-risk patients before symptoms occur; and has adaptive algorithms that incorporate clinical data, claims, and socioeconomic figures ([8]: p. 2).

A recent study examined the effects of clinical decision-support systems (CDSSs) on practitioner performance and patient outcomes. Clinical decision-support tools made available to practitioners and patients, such as computer-generated clinical knowledge and patient-related information, were studied. When such data are filtered and made available at appropriate times, it was shown to enhance patient care. CDSS can also send reminders, warnings, test results, check for drug interactions, dosage errors, contraindications, and list patients eligible for specific interventions such as immunizations and follow-ups [9].

The study found that CDSSs that require large amounts of data entry adversely affect physician satisfaction and use of the system. When large amounts of data required for the CDSS to be effective are incomplete, diagnoses will be less accurate, or it will take longer to complete the data, resulting in delays in the CDSS to accurately deliver advice. Anticoagulant-prescribing CDSSs are a case in point; the data required are more complex and have a higher patient variance.

CDSSs requiring limited number of patient data items for input were the most used and clinically successful. Examples include preventative care reminder systems for routine tasks such as blood pressure tests, pap smears, vaccinations, etc.

The study concluded that CDSSs become more effective as they become more specified and sensitive in their levels of advice but at the same time the manual input of data needs to be minimized, and the CDSS advice needs to be available in a timely manner to be of relevance for physician use.

6. Advanced genetic technologies

Personalized medicine is making an impact in advanced genetic technologies as well. Genome modulation (modifications), in particular, has an array of applications, from energy, food, and industrial to medical. Researchers are turning to genome modulation with the hope that it will provide the key to understanding and answering some of life's most difficult and challenging questions.

Genome modulation applied medically has been known as gene therapy, but with new technologies, has evolved into the science of gene editing. At the forefront of this technology is what is now known as Clustered Regularly Interspaced Short Palindromic Repeats, or CRISPR. Experts claim CRISPR has brought with it new streams of business based on its cutting-edge technologies [10].

One recent example of CRISPR technology application is the correction of blood clotting problems in newborn and adult mice, with marked success. The aim is to cure the majority of patients with hemophilia B with CRISPR-based gene targeting [10].

Growing interest in CRISPR technology is speeding its transition to research, clinical trials, and applications in humans, and it was recently tested on a human being for the first time. In China, a patient diagnosed with terminal lung cancer was treated with CRISPR gene editing therapy as part of a clinical trial. Meanwhile, clinical trials in the United States using CRISPR technology are underway.

CRISPR technology has opened channels for business, but there are still many daunting challenges before its application can be realized clinically. One such hurdle, if not the most significant one, is regulation. Personalized medicine, including gene editing technologies, is involved in a regulatory business, involving peer-reviewed, published papers and clinical trials. Even in cooperation with the FDA, for example, it could still take a new technology 20 years to be approved.

7. Robotics and advanced medical devices

Another way in which personalized medicine is driven by advancements in technology is in healthcare robotics. The introduction of robotics in healthcare is driven by the desire to improve quality, safety, and control expenditure. Surgical robots, service robots, companion robots, cognitive therapy robots, robotic limbs and exoskeletons, humanoids, and rehabilitation robots are just a few applied areas already making use of this technology.

Despite clear advantages and a promising, growing future of robotics in healthcare and in medical devices, there is a need for a robotics strategy that addresses concerns and challenges. Patient and cultural perceptions, liability rules, and ethical debates present challenges to the integration and development of robotics in healthcare.

A recent study suggested that a deliberative approach is needed to find a balance between developing overarching rules in this industry and allowing innovation to flourish, and that robots and robotic devices should be viewed as "augmenting human capabilities and empowering professionals in their role" so that patients would have a more positive perception of robotics in their healthcare settings [11].

Another recent study suggests that robotics lags behind its healthcare potential primarily because the industry has yet to live up to a primary principle of Cybernetics. According to this theory, robots and robotic devices should have a high level of adaptation and reaction to environments, resulting in complete interaction between humans and robots [12]. In this study, robotics-assisted surgery, rehabilitation, prosthetics, and companion systems were analyzed.

In all areas, the study concluded, for one, that the real potential of robotics in these fields requires a much greater degree of customization. Customization is defined as the robotic technology's adaptation to clinicians and patients, and the authors argue that existing robotic systems are limited in their ability for customization, which greatly limits its practical use in healthcare. The idea is that technology should adapt to users, rather than forcing users to adapt to technology.

Despite implicit or even explicit claims of the superiority of robotic systems for healthcare, when compared to more traditional methods, the clear advantage of these systems is currently unproven and highly dependent on the skills of the users. Therefore, the success of such technologies is still heavily dependent on adequate training and experience.

8. 3D printing drugs

As our last example in this chapter of the impact of technology in medicine, consider the "3D" printing (3DP) of oral drugs. While it may sound novel and revolutionary, drug manufacturing using 3DP technology is actually a combination of well-established technologies first developed to meet the needs of engineering prototypes [13], namely building objects by creating sequentially added layers.

There are a few driving forces behind the 3DP of oral drugs: personalization, on-demand capability, and the ability to manufacture drugs in new, decentralized locations. A recent study suggests that the key to the success of utilizing 3DP technology for healthcare and medicine is to maximize patient benefits while providing production efficiency, and that 3DP has a proven track record. As such, they argue, its future is clearly viable in three fields, namely preclinical, within a pharmaceutics framework; innovative drug delivery concepts; and decentralizing the drug manufacturing process [13].

Although this technology is currently niche and not an alternative to mainstream mass production processes, there is a clear place for 3DP in healthcare and medicine and its role will be more clearly defined in the future by incorporating considerations such as ideal population product profile, drug formulation, and engineering, as well as the management of regulatory and supply chain factors [13].

9. How to engage the patient to the human-machine innovation?

Due to the technological advances described above along with the growing need for smarter, preventive, more accurate, and effective medicine, the healthcare industry is advancing into the digital age—the digital health revolution. The digital health revolution is made possible by advances in medical information technologies—information storage, data analysis, mobile, sensors, and genetic information. All this will enable the capture and analysis of vast amounts of information about patients, populations, environments, and the lifestyle in which they live, and thus adapt personalized treatment accordingly.

The technological advances facilitating personalized medicine enable the capture of major challenges of the health system and chronic diseases [3]. The reason that chronic diseases are the major financial burden on the healthcare system is because most chronic disorders develop outside healthcare settings, and patients with these conditions require continuous interventions to make behavioral and lifestyles changes needed to effectively manage the disease.

The challenge with chronic diseases is the transition from health to disease with late-onset symptoms that can be irreversible. Coincidentally, the majority of chronic diseases can be prevented or delayed in life through interventions as described above, which results in an extended health span (the duration of individual life spent in a state of wellness, free of disease). Current chronic disease management is characterized by fragmented interventions and communication and recommendations from specialists, becoming constitutive only following the onset of disease symptoms. At the stage where an individual is free of symptoms, preventive activities management is done mostly by individuals themselves.

Due to the growing evidence that links patients' activation, defined as the patients' willingness and ability to take independent actions to manage their health and care, to their health and cost outcomes, methods and tools need to be developed to increase patient activation and engagement to accelerate the needed behavior change.

Encompassing both the design thinking approach and behavioral economics can motivate people to change their current behavioral health-related habits to improve their health. This underscores the need to devise a personalized, preventive medical infrastructure with recommendations and motivation mechanisms taken from behavioral economics.

Behavioral economics aims at realizing the human irrational decision process underpinning suboptimal outcomes, which in our context translates to unhealthy behavior patterns. In recent years, government agencies around the world have been employing behavioral economics models and methods as complementing means to standard public-policy tools that are implemented by decision-makers. These measures, based on the "Nudge" theory [14], are used for preventing policy-implementation failures and positively impacting motivation and decision-making by individuals and groups. Thus far, this theory has inspired a variety of applications in areas such as education, health, safety and environment. Extensive applied research, performed in the UK by the Department for Environment, Food & Rural Affairs [15], has outlined nine principles influencing human behavior, based on research in social psychology and behavioral economics.

Integrating elements from persuasive technologies for supporting extrinsic motivation factors stemming from communication and social aspects, such as incentives and norms, will have a great impact on the implantation and engagement of the patient. These technologies provide effective means for supporting the operationalization of "Nudge" theory, for example by producing email messages for raising awareness regarding fulfillment of required assignments, delivering informative messages related to the performance of these assignments, and promoting a climate that reflects social norms within online social networks. Studies have shown that nudging could also incorporate various approaches that focus on changing physical or social environments to increase the likelihood of certain behaviors. This could include the provision of social norm feedback, which will increase the likelihood of healthy behaviors, altering the defaults surrounding how food and drinks are served, or even changing the layout of buildings to encourage physical activity ([16]: p. 263). Nudging focuses on a set of simple and low-cost remedies that may not require any legislation and can be used to solve most of the problems emanating from human contact. On the other hand, nudging could also enhance behaviors that may worsen the health of individuals ([16]: p. 264). For instance, food products may be labeled as healthy, hence causing consumers to ignore the energy content, which may lead to excessive consumption of such products.

The value of technologies that increase patient activation and engagement is paramount due to the increasing incidence of chronic diseases. Therefore, developing "patient-centered" technologies will increase adoption and diffusion of these technologies.

Author details

Neta Kela-Madar[1]* and Itai Kela[2]

1 The Sami Shamoon College of Engineering, Ashdod, Israel

2 Israel Innovation Authority, Jerusalem, Israel

*Address all correspondence to: neta.kela@gmail.com

References

[1] Embracing the future of work to unlock R&D productivity. Deloitte. 2018. Available from: https://www2.deloitte.com/uk/en/pages/life-sciences-and-healthcare/articles/measuring-return-from-pharmaceutical-innovation.html

[2] Sagner M, McNeil A, Puska P, et al. The P4 health spectrum—A predictive, preventive, personalized and participatory continuum for promoting healthspan. Progress in Cardiovascular Diseases. 2016;**59**(5):506-521

[3] Kvedar JC. Digital medicine's march on chronic disease. Nature Biotechnology. 2016;**34**:239-246

[4] Dilsizian ME, Siegel EL. Machine meets biology: A primer on artificial intelligence in cardiology and cardiac imaging. Current Cardiology Reports. 2018;**20**:139

[5] Frölich H et al. From Hype to Reality: Data Science Enabling Personalized Medicine. 2018. DOI: 10.1186/s12916-018-1122-7 [Online]

[6] Allen LN, Christie GP. The emergence of personalized health technology. Journal of Medical Internet Research. 2016;**18**(5):e99

[7] Phillips MA, Harrington TS, Srai JS. Convergent innovation in emerging healthcare technology ecosystems: Addressing complexity and integration. Technology and Innovation Management Review. 2017;7(9):44

[8] Ainslie J. An Epidemic of Misdiagnosis: Using AI to Solve a Quiet Crisis in Healthcare. USA: Aibusiness, Texas; 2018. p. 1

[9] Jaspers MWM, Smeulers M, Vermeulen H, Peute LW. Effects of clinical decision-support systems on practitioner performance and patient outcomes: A synthesis of high-quality systematic review findings. Journal of the American Medical Informatics Association. 2011;**18**:327-334

[10] Stangelli J. CRISPR Tech Heralds Hype, Hope, and Hurdles for Gene-Based Therapeutics. 2016. Available from: http://www.bio-itworld.com/2016/12/12/crispr-tech-heralds-hype-hope-and-hurdlesfor-gene-based-therapeutics-or-how-to-cure-cancer-and-aids-with-this-one-weirdtrick.aspx [Accessed: Dec. 20, 2016, in Bio-ITWorld: Online]

[11] Cresswell K, Cunningham-Burley S, Sheikh A. Health care robotics: qualitative exploration of key challenges and future directions. Journal of Medical Internet Research. 2018;**20**(7):e10410. DOI: 10.2196/10410

[12] Andrade AO, Pereira AA, Walter S, Almeida R, Loureiro R, Compagna D, et al. Bridging the gap between robotic technology and health care. Biomedical Signal Processing and Control. 2014;**10**:65-78

[13] Hsiao WK, Lorber B, Reitsamer H, Khinast J. 3D printing of oral drugs: a new reality or hype? Expert Opinion On Drug Delivery. 2018;**15**(1):1-4. DOI: 10.1080/17425247.2017.1371698

[14] Thaler RH, Sunstein CB. Nudge. New Haven, CT: Yale University Press; 2008

[15] Department for Environment, Food, and Rural Affairs. A Framework for Proenvironmental Behaviours. 2008. Available from: www.defra.gov.uk

[16] Roland M, Kelly PM, Suhrcke M. Judging nudging: Can nudging improve population health? BMJ. 2011;**342**:263-265